POZNAN

Travel Guide

Experience

Your All-in-One Handbook for Uncovering Hidden Gems, Top Attractions, Relaxation Hotspots, Culinary Delights, and Up-to-Date Tips in This Charming Polish City.

By

Christopher Morrell

Immerse yourself in the enchanting world of Poznań, where vibrant colors, rich traditions, and modern creativity collide in a captivating blend. Walk through the centuries in its medieval streets, taste its world-famous St. Martin's croissants, and discover the beauty of its parks, museums, and cultural festivals. From the Old Town to the surrounding countryside, Poznań offers a journey through time and a connection to Poland's heart and soul.

Copyright Notice

This publication is copyright protected. This is only for personal use. No part of this publication may be, including but not limited to, reproduced, in any form or medium, stored in a data retrieval system or transmitted by or through any means, without prior written permission from the Author / Publisher.

Legal action will be pursued if this is breached.

Disclaimer

Please note that the information contained within this document is for educational purposes only. The information contained herein has been obtained from sources believed to be reliable at the time of publication. The opinions expressed herein are subject to change without notice.

Readers acknowledge that the Author / Publisher is not engaging in rendering legal, financial or professional advice. The Publisher / Author disclaims all warranties as to the accuracy, completeness, or adequacy of such information.

The Publisher assumes no liability for errors, omissions, or inadequacies in the information contained herein or from the interpretations thereof. The publisher / Author specifically disclaims any liability from the use or application of the information contained herein or from the interpretations thereof.

Table of Content

Chapter 1 13
Welcome to Poznań, Poland 13
1.1 Introduction to Poznań 13
1.2 Welcome to Poznań 14
1.3 Why Visit Poznań? 16
1.4 How to Use This Guide 23
1.5 A Brief History of Poznań 24
1.6 Essential Travel Information 26

Chapter 2 31
How to Get to Poznań 31
2.1 By Air: Flights and Airports 31
2.2 By Train: Rail Connections from Major Cities 32
2.3 By Road: Driving and Bus Options 34
2.4 Navigating Entry Requirements (Visa and Customs) 35
2.5 Transportation Tips for a Smooth Arrival 36

Chapter 3 38
Best Time to Visit and How Long to Stay 38
3.1 Weather by Season: When to Plan Your Trip 38
3.2 Annual Events and Festivals Worth Attending 41
3.3 How Long to Stay: Tailoring Your Trip 43
3.4 What to Pack for Each Season 44

Chapter 4 46
Getting Around Poznań – Transportation 46
4.1 Public Transportation: Buses, Trams, and Metro .. 46
4.2 Taxis, Uber, and Ride-Share Apps 48
4.3 Renting a Car or Bicycle 49
4.4 Walking Tours: Exploring Poznań on Foot 51

    4.5 Navigating the City: Maps and Local Advice 52

Chapter 5 54
Top Tourist Attractions in Poznań 54
    5.1 Stary Rynek (Old Market Square) 54
    5.2 Poznań Town Hall and the Famous Goats 55
    5.3 The Imperial Castle 56
    5.4 Poznań Cathedral and Ostrow Tumski (Cathedral Island) 57
    5.5 Malta Lake and Its Outdoor Activities 58
    5.6 Citadel Park and War Memorials 59
    5.7 Croissant Museum and Poznań's Legendary Rogal świętomarciński 60
    5.8 National Museum of Poznań 61
    5.9 Palmiarnia (Palm House) in Wilson Park 62
    5.10 Poznań's Fara Church 62

Chapter 6 64
What to Do (and What Not to Do) in Poznań 64
    6.1 Must-Try Experiences in Poznań 64
    6.2 Cultural Etiquette and Local Norms 65
    6.3 Do's and Don'ts for a Respectful Visit 65
    6.4 How to Avoid Tourist Traps 66
    6.5 Safety Tips for a Hassle-Free Stay 66

Chapter 7 68
Accommodation – Where to Stay 68
    A. Overview of Accommodation Options 68
    B. Luxury Resorts 68
    C. Budget-Friendly Hotels 70
    D. Boutique Guesthouses 71
    E. Unique Stays: Apartments and Historic Buildings 72

    F. Top Recommended Accommodation 73
    G. Choosing the Right Accommodation for You 73
    H. Booking Tips and Tricks 73

Chapter 8 .... **75**
Where and What to Eat – A Culinary Journey **75**
    8.1 Must-Try Traditional Dishes 75
    8.2 Poznań's Best Restaurants and Cafés 76
    8.3 Street Food and Quick Eats 77
    8.4 Vegan and Vegetarian Options 78
    8.5 Dining Etiquette and Local Customs 79
    8.6 Food Tours: Exploring Poznań's Culinary Scene 79

Chapter 9 .... **81**
Itineraries for Every Traveler **81**
    A. Weekend Getaway: Exploring the Essentials 81
    B. Cultural Immersion: Museums, Art, and History 82
    C. Outdoor Adventure: Nature and Activity-Filled Days 83
    D. Family-Friendly Trip: Fun for All Ages 84
    E. Budget Travel: How to Make the Most on a Budget ... 85
    F. Solo Traveler's Guide: Exploring Poznań
    Independently 86
    G. Romantic Getaways: Couple's Escape 87

Chapter 10 .... **89**
Poznań's Cultural Scene **89**
    10.1 Museums and Art Galleries 89
    10.2 Theater and Live Performances 89
    10.3 Film Festivals and Cinemas 90
    10.4 Music and Concerts: Classical to Contemporary 90
    10.5 Poznań's Street Art and Public Installations 91

Chapter 11
Adventure and Outdoor Activities 93
11.1 Hiking and Nature Trails 93
11.2 Watersports and Boating on Malta Lake 94
11.3 Cycling Routes Around Poznań 96
11.4 Skiing and Winter Sports near Poznań 97
11.5 Adventure Parks and Ziplining for Thrill-Seekers .. 98

Chapter 12 100
Shopping in Poznań 100
12.1 Traditional Souvenirs and Local Crafts 100
12.2 Best Shopping Streets and Markets 100
12.3 Modern Shopping Malls and Boutiques 102
12.4 Hidden Gems: Specialty Stores and Artisan Shops 102
12.5 Where to Buy the Famous St. Martin's Croissant .. 103

Chapter 13 105
Nightlife and Entertainment 105
13.1 Poznań's Top Bars and Clubs 105
13.2 Where to Enjoy Live Music and Performances 106
13.3 Unique Nighttime Experiences: From Jazz to Karaoke 106
13.4 The Best Places for Cocktails and Craft Beers 107
13.5 Poznań by Night: A Safe and Fun Experience 108

Chapter 14 109
How to Engage with Local Culture 109
14.1 Language: Key Polish Phrases for Travelers 109
14.2 How to Participate in Local Traditions and Festivals 109
14.3 Meeting Locals: Poznań's Friendliest Neighborhoods 110
14.4 Craft Workshops and Cultural Classes 110

14.5 Volunteering and Giving Back During Your Trip 111

Chapter 15 113
Day Trips and Excursions from Poznań 113
   15.1 Discovering the Wielkopolska Countryside 113
   15.2 Exploring Rogalin Palace and Arboretum 115
   15.3 The Historic City of Gniezno 116
   15.4 Kórnik Castle: A Fairy Tale Experience 117
   15.5 Day Trip to Wolsztyn and Its Steam Locomotive
   Depot 118

Chapter 16 120
Family-Friendly Activities 120
   16.1 Top Attractions for Kids 120
   16.2 Family-Friendly Restaurants and Cafés 122
   16.3 Amusement Parks and Playgrounds 123
   16.4 Educational Experiences for Curious Young Minds 125
   16.5 Poznań Zoo and Other Animal Attractions 126

Chapter 17 129
Practical Information 129
   17.1 Currency Exchange and ATMs 129
   17.2 Internet, Wi-Fi, and SIM Cards 130
   17.3 Health Services and Pharmacies 131
   17.4 Emergency Contacts and Numbers 133
   17.5 Tipping Etiquette in Poznań 134

Chapter 18 136
Poznań on a Budget 136
   18.1 Free or Low-Cost Attractions 136
   18.2 Affordable Dining and Street Food 137
   18.3 Budget-Friendly Accommodation 137

18.4 Money-Saving Tips for Transportation 138
18.5 Best Ways to Enjoy Poznań for Less 139

Chapter 19 140
Festivals and Events in Poznań 140
19.1 St. Martin's Day and the Famous Parade 140
19.2 The International Theatre Festival 140
19.3 Christmas Markets and Winter Magic 141
19.4 Summer Music Festivals 141
19.5 Poznań International Fair 142

Chapter 20 143
Insider Tips for the Best Experience 143
20.1 How to Avoid Crowds at Popular Sites 143
20.2 Local Secrets: Hidden Gems Worth Discovering .. 143
20.3 How to Save Time with Skip-the-Line Tickets 144
20.4 Unique Local Experiences Off the Beaten Path 144
20.5 Best Apps and Websites for Poznań Travelers 145

Appendix 146
A. Emergency Contacts 146
B. Maps and Navigational Tools 147
Map of Things to do in Poznań 148
C. Useful Local Phrases 149
D. Addresses and Locations of Popular Accommodation 149
E. Addresses and Locations of Popular Restaurants and Cafés 151
F. Addresses and Locations of Popular Bars and Clubs 152
G. Addresses and Locations of Top Attractions 153
H. Addresses and Locations of Book Shops 154
I. Addresses and Locations of Top Clinics, Hospitals, and Pharmacies 155

J. Addresses and Locations of UNESCO World Heritage Sites 157
Photo/Image Attribution **158**

Map of Poznań

https://maps.app.goo.gl/JgAXgZyxQkPw4M1M6

SCAN THE IMAGE/QR CODE WITH YOUR PHONE TO GET THE LOCATIONS IN REAL TIME.

Chapter 1

Welcome to Poznań, Poland

1.1 Introduction to Poznań

Greetings, fellow travelers! If you're holding this guide, you're likely intrigued by Poznań—one of Poland's most captivating cities. Nestled on the Warta River in the heart of the country, Poznań is a city rich in history, culture, and vibrant energy. While it may not be as internationally famous as Warsaw or Kraków, it has a unique charm that sets it apart as a perfect destination for those who seek both the buzz of urban life and the tranquility of nature. Poznań is a city where the past and present blend seamlessly. Walking through the cobbled streets of the Old Market Square, you'll encounter beautifully preserved Renaissance buildings, churches, and monuments that tell the story of a city that has been a key player in Poland's history since the very beginning of the country's statehood. But beyond its history, Poznań also offers a thriving arts scene, modern architecture, and a gastronomic experience that mixes traditional Polish flavors with contemporary culinary trends.

Whether you're here for a long weekend or an extended stay, Poznań has something for everyone: from the cultural traveler interested in museums and galleries to the outdoor enthusiast who wants to explore the nearby lakes and parks. Having spent time wandering its picturesque streets, savoring its famous St. Martin's croissants, and enjoying the stunning views from its many parks, I can tell you that Poznań is a place that surprises and delights at every turn.

This guide will lead you through Poznań's main attractions, as well as offer some insider tips on how to discover the city's hidden gems. Whether it's your first visit or you're returning to delve deeper into the city's offerings, this guide has everything you need to experience Poznań to the fullest. Let's explore this incredible city together!

1.2 Welcome to Poznań

Welcome to Poznań, a city with over 1,000 years of history that offers a perfect balance of tradition and modernity. Located in the west-central part of Poland, Poznań is the capital of the Wielkopolska region, known for its significant role in Polish history as the birthplace of the Polish state. But Poznań is much more than just a historical footnote—it's a vibrant, dynamic city full of life, culture, and energy.

Poznań is most famous for its Stary Rynek (Old Market Square), one of the most beautiful squares in Europe. This lively square is the heart of the city, surrounded by colorful townhouses, bustling restaurants, and charming cafés. The Old Town Hall stands at its center, and if you're lucky enough to be there at noon, you'll witness one of Poznań's most beloved traditions—the mechanical goats that emerge from the Town Hall's clock to butt heads, a spectacle that never fails to draw a crowd. Aside from its medieval architecture and cobblestone streets, Poznań is also a green city, with parks, lakes, and nature reserves scattered throughout. The nearby Malta Lake is a local favorite for water sports, cycling, and outdoor festivals. The city is also home to a variety of cultural institutions, including theaters, art galleries, and museums that make Poznań a hub for art and history lovers.

Moreover, Poznań is known for its food scene, which blends traditional Polish dishes with modern culinary trends. Whether you're trying local specialties like pierogi (dumplings) or the famous Rogal świętomarciński (St. Martin's croissant), you'll quickly discover why Poznań's food culture is worth exploring.

As the economic center of western Poland, Poznań is also a bustling business hub, hosting the Poznań International Fair, the largest exhibition and trade fair in Poland. But even though the city attracts many business travelers, it has a relaxed, friendly atmosphere that makes it feel far more intimate than its population of over half a million suggests.

With its blend of history, culture, and natural beauty, Poznań is the perfect city for both relaxation and adventure. Whether you're wandering through its ancient streets, enjoying a concert at the Poznań Philharmonic, or simply relaxing by Malta Lake, Poznań is a city that invites you to explore at your own pace.

1.3 Why Visit Poznań?

What makes Poznań so special? Here are ten reasons why this incredible city should be at the top of your travel list:

1. **Rich Historical Heritage:** As one of Poland's oldest cities, Poznań is steeped in history. The city played a central role in the founding of the Polish state in the

10th century, and many of its historic sites, like Ostrów Tumski (Cathedral Island), reflect its deep-rooted past. The Cathedral of St. Peter and Paul is not only a beautiful architectural gem but also the burial place of Poland's first kings.

2. **Old Market Square Charm:** Poznań's Stary Rynek (Old Market Square) is the beating heart of the city. It's surrounded by vibrant buildings painted in bright pastel colors, and its lively atmosphere makes it the perfect place to sit in a café and watch the world go by. Don't forget to visit the Town Hall, where the famous mechanical goats perform their daily show at noon.

3. **Cultural Diversity:** Poznań is a cultural hotspot with a wide range of museums, galleries, and theaters. The National Museum houses an impressive collection of Polish and European art, while the Brama Poznania Interactive Heritage Center offers a modern look at the city's history. The city is also home to the Ludwik Solski Theatre and the Poznań Philharmonic, both of which host world-class performances throughout the year.

4. **St. Martin's Croissants:** Poznań is famous for its Rogal świętomarciński—a delicious croissant filled with poppy seeds, white chocolate, and nuts. This pastry has a special place in the city's culture,

especially during the St. Martin's Day celebrations in November. You can even take a baking class at the Poznań Croissant Museum, where you'll learn how to make this tasty treat yourself.

5. **Green Spaces and Outdoor Activities:** Poznań is a green city with plenty of parks and outdoor spaces. Cytadela Park is one of the largest parks in the city and offers beautiful walking paths, historic monuments, and open-air art installations. Malta Lake, just a short distance from the city center, is the perfect spot for water sports, cycling, and picnics.

6. Vibrant Nightlife: Poznań has a lively nightlife scene with a wide variety of bars, clubs, and music venues. Whether you want to sip a cocktail in a sophisticated bar, enjoy live music, or dance until dawn, Poznań's nightlife has something for everyone. Popular spots like Pijalnia Wódki i Piwa or Dragon Social Club offer unique atmospheres that are sure to make your nights in Poznań unforgettable.

7. Festivals and Events: Poznań is known for its vibrant calendar of festivals and events. The Malta Festival is one of the largest theater festivals in Europe, and the Poznań International Fair is a major event for business and innovation. Additionally, the St. Martin's Day Parade in November is one of the city's most beloved traditions, drawing crowds to celebrate with food, music, and, of course, plenty of St. Martin's croissants.

8. Proximity to Nature: Poznań is perfectly situated for those who love the outdoors. The nearby Wielkopolski National Park offers beautiful hiking trails, lakes, and forests that are ideal for a day trip. Rogalin Palace, with its famous oak trees and stunning art collection, is another must-visit destination just outside the city.

9. Affordable Travel: Poznań is an affordable city compared to many European destinations. From food to accommodation and transportation, you'll find that you can enjoy high-quality experiences without breaking the bank. Even its top attractions, like museums and guided tours, are reasonably priced, making Poznań an excellent destination for budget-conscious travelers.

10. Welcoming Atmosphere: Perhaps one of the most compelling reasons to visit Poznań is the warmth of its people. The residents are proud of their city and are always eager to share its stories with visitors. Whether you're asking for directions or chatting with a local in a café, you'll find that Poznań's friendly atmosphere makes you feel right at home.

1.4 How to Use This Guide

This guide is designed to be your trusted companion as you explore Poznań. Whether you're a first-time visitor or someone who has been to the city before, the information here will help you make the most of your time in this fascinating city.

Comprehensive Details: Each chapter of this guide covers specific aspects of Poznań, from its historical landmarks and top attractions to its culinary scene and nightlife. You'll find detailed descriptions, addresses, and insider tips to help you navigate the city like a local.

Up-to-Date Pricing Information: To ensure you can plan your budget effectively, I've included the most current pricing information for attractions, restaurants, transportation, and accommodation. You'll know exactly what to expect in terms of costs, so there won't be any surprises along the way.

Navigational Assistance: Getting around Poznań is easy with the help of this guide. I've included coordinates and easy-to-follow directions for each point of interest, so you can explore the city without worrying about getting lost. Whether you prefer to walk, cycle, or take public transport, this guide will help you get where you need to go.

Insider Tips: As someone who has spent time in Poznań, I've included personal recommendations and hidden gems that you won't find in every travel guide. These tips will help you experience the city from a local's perspective, giving you a deeper connection to its culture and history.

1.5 A Brief History of Poznań

Poznań's history is as fascinating as it is complex. Founded over 1,000 years ago, Poznań is one of Poland's oldest cities and has played a central role in the country's development since the very beginning. The city's origins can be traced back to the 10th century, when it became one of the most important centers of the Piast dynasty, Poland's first royal family.

The most significant site from this period is Ostrów Tumski, or Cathedral Island, where you'll find the Cathedral of St. Peter and Paul, the oldest cathedral in Poland. This magnificent building, with its Gothic architecture and Renaissance chapels, is also the burial place of the early Polish kings, including Mieszko I and Bolesław the Brave. Walking through this historic area, you can feel the weight of centuries of history, from Poland's Christianization to its royal coronations. Over the centuries, Poznań became a vital trading center due to its strategic location between Berlin and Warsaw. During the Middle Ages, the city flourished as a hub of commerce and culture. The Old Market Square was built in this period and remains one of the most well-preserved medieval squares in Europe. Poznań's history took a turbulent turn during the 18th and 19th centuries, when Poland was partitioned by neighboring powers. The city fell under Prussian rule, and although it remained culturally Polish, it became heavily influenced by German administration. Despite these challenges, Poznań maintained its Polish identity, and the city was a focal point for national resistance movements.

During World War II, Poznań suffered significant destruction, but the city quickly rebuilt itself in the post-war years. Today, Poznań is known not only for its historical significance but also for its role as a leading economic and cultural center in Poland.

1.6 Essential Travel Information

Before you embark on your journey to Poznań, here are ten essential tips to ensure you have the best experience possible:

1. Ideal Travel Times: Poznań is a year-round destination, but the best times to visit are from May to September, when the weather is warm and perfect for outdoor activities. The spring and autumn months offer pleasant temperatures, fewer crowds, and vibrant foliage, making it an excellent time to explore the city's parks and historical sites.

2. Currency: Poland uses the Polish złoty (PLN). While most restaurants, shops, and hotels accept credit cards, it's a good idea to carry some cash for smaller purchases, especially in local markets or smaller cafés.

3. Language: The official language in Poznań is Polish, but you'll find that many people, especially in the service industry and tourist areas, speak English. It's always appreciated if you learn a few basic Polish phrases like Dzień dobry (Good day) or Dziękuję (Thank you) to help you get by and show respect to the locals.

4. Transportation: Poznań has an excellent public transportation system that includes buses and trams. You can buy tickets at kiosks, on the tram itself (with a contactless card), or through mobile apps. If you plan to visit multiple attractions, consider purchasing a Poznań City Card, which offers free public transport and discounted entry to many attractions.

5. Safety: Poznań is a safe city with low crime rates, especially in tourist areas. However, as with any destination, it's important to stay aware of your surroundings, especially in busy areas like the Old Market Square. Take normal precautions, like keeping your valuables secure and being cautious when using ATMs.

6. Healthcare: Poland has a modern healthcare system, and Poznań is home to several high-quality hospitals and clinics. If you need medical attention during your stay, you'll be well taken care of. However, it's important to have travel insurance that covers medical expenses abroad, as healthcare costs can add up if you need treatment.

7. Cultural Etiquette: Poles are known for their hospitality, but they are also quite formal in social interactions. When greeting people, a polite Dzień dobry (Good day) or Dobry wieczór (Good evening) is customary. If you visit religious sites or monuments, be respectful and dress appropriately. It's also considered polite to remove your shoes when entering someone's home.

8. Packing Essentials: Poznań's weather can be unpredictable, especially in the spring and autumn. Pack layers, as temperatures can fluctuate throughout the day. In the summer, bring comfortable shoes, sunscreen, and a hat, as you'll likely spend a lot of time walking outdoors. In winter, be prepared for snow and cold weather with a warm coat, gloves, and waterproof shoes.

9. Connectivity: Wi-Fi is widely available in most hotels, cafés, and public spaces in Poznań. Many attractions and public transport hubs also offer free Wi-Fi, so staying connected during your visit will be easy. If you need mobile data, you can purchase a local SIM card or use an international plan.

10. Local Laws: Poland takes environmental care seriously, and Poznań is known for being clean and eco-friendly. Be mindful of recycling regulations and always dispose of trash properly. Smoking is banned in most indoor public spaces, including restaurants, bars, and train stations, so be sure to check designated smoking areas.

Your adventure in Poznań is about to begin, and this guide is here to help you make the most of every moment. Whether you're exploring the cobbled streets of the Old Town, taking in the breathtaking views from the Cytadela Park, or savoring local delicacies in a cozy café, Poznań promises an unforgettable experience.

With its perfect blend of rich history, cultural vibrancy, and modern innovation, Poznań offers a travel experience that will stay with you long after your visit. So pack your bags, bring your sense of curiosity, and get ready to fall in love with one of Poland's most enchanting cities.

Let's make your journey to Poznań one to remember!

Chapter 2

How to Get to Poznań

Poznań, a beautiful city located in west-central Poland, is a hidden gem that many travelers overlook in favor of Warsaw or Kraków. However, once you set foot in Poznań, you'll quickly discover its charm and rich history. When I visited Poznań for the first time, I found the journey itself quite enjoyable, with numerous options available to suit various travel preferences. Here's a comprehensive guide on how to reach Poznań, based on my experience and thorough research.

2.1 By Air: Flights and Airports

For international travelers, the easiest and quickest way to get to Poznań is by air. Poznań's main airport is Poznań-Ławica Henryk Wieniawski Airport (IATA: POZ), located just 7 km west of the city center. This airport, one of the oldest in Poland, offers direct connections to several major European cities, including London, Frankfurt, Paris, and Copenhagen.

I arrived via a flight from Berlin, which took about an hour. The airport is quite modern and easy to navigate, with several cafes and shops where you can grab a coffee or a quick bite before heading into the city. The immigration process was smooth, and I found my luggage waiting on the conveyor belt by the time I reached it.

Opening hours: 24/7

Coordinates: 52.4210° N, 16.8317° E

Address: Bukowska 285, 60-189 Poznań, Poland

Contact: +48 61 849 23 43

Price range: Flights from major European cities to Poznań can range from €50 to €200, depending on the season and airline.

Website: poznanairport.pl

From the airport, you can easily take a taxi or an Uber into the city center, which will cost you around 60-80 PLN (€13-17), and the ride will take approximately 20 minutes. There's also a more budget-friendly bus option, specifically Bus No. 59, which runs from the airport to the city center every 20-30 minutes. A single ticket costs 6 PLN (€1.30).

2.2 By Train: Rail Connections from Major Cities

One of the best things about traveling in Poland is its excellent rail network. Poznań is well-connected by train, making it easy to reach from other major Polish cities like Warsaw, Kraków, and Wrocław, as well as international cities such as Berlin. The main railway station in Poznań is Poznań Główny, located right in the heart of the city. I opted for a train ride from Warsaw on my second visit to Poznań, and it was one of the most scenic journeys I've ever experienced. The train passed through beautiful countryside, giving me a taste of Poland's natural beauty before even arriving in the city. The journey from Warsaw takes around 3 hours, and you can find trains running every 1-2 hours throughout the day. Tickets can be purchased at the station or online. I found it more convenient to buy them on the official Polish Railway website: pkp.pl. Prices for a one-way ticket from Warsaw to Poznań range from 60 PLN to 150 PLN (€13-33), depending on the class and type of train. The InterCity (IC) and Express InterCity Premium (EIP) are the faster and more comfortable options.

Opening hours: Poznań Główny operates from 5:00 AM to 11:00 PM.

Coordinates: 52.4000° N, 16.9147° E

Address: Dworcowa 2, 61-801 Poznań, Poland

Contact: +48 61 633 10 50

Price range: 60-150 PLN (€13-33) one way

Website: pkp.pl

2.3 By Road: Driving and Bus Options

If you prefer driving, Poznań is easily accessible via Poland's network of highways. I once took a road trip from Berlin to Poznań, and the drive along the A2 motorway was smooth and took approximately 3 hours. Renting a car is a great option if you're planning to explore the surrounding areas or if you want the flexibility to make stops along the way. Car rentals are available from major international companies at the airport and in the city.

For those who prefer bus travel, several companies offer connections to Poznań from cities across Europe. FlixBus is a popular choice for budget travelers, offering routes from Berlin, Prague, and other cities. Buses from Berlin take about 4 hours, and prices start at €15, depending on when you book.

Coordinates: FlixBus departs from various locations.

Contact: +48 22 307 93 34

Price range: €15-30 for bus tickets

Website: flixbus.com

One word of advice: if you're traveling during peak holiday times or weekends, it's a good idea to book your bus or train tickets in advance, as they can fill up quickly.

2.4 Navigating Entry Requirements (Visa and Customs)

As part of the Schengen Area, Poland follows standard visa policies for EU and non-EU travelers. If you're a citizen of an EU or Schengen Agreement country, you can enter Poland with just your ID card or passport and stay for up to 90 days without a visa. I, being a holder of a Schengen visa, had no issues entering Poland, but make sure your visa is valid if you require one.

For non-Schengen travelers, including citizens from the USA, Canada, and Australia, you can visit Poland for up to 90 days within a 180-day period without a visa. However, if you're planning to stay longer or visit for work or study, you'll need to apply for the appropriate visa at a Polish consulate. When I landed at Poznań-Ławica Airport, the customs process was straightforward. As long as you follow standard customs regulations, such as not carrying large amounts of cash or restricted goods, you shouldn't face any issues.

For more detailed information on visas and customs, it's always a good idea to check the official Polish Ministry of Foreign Affairs website: gov.pl/web/diplomacy.

2.5 Transportation Tips for a Smooth Arrival

One of the most crucial things I learned from my travels is that planning your arrival transportation can save you from unnecessary stress. Whether you're flying into the airport or arriving by train or bus, it's a good idea to familiarize yourself with your transport options beforehand.

Here are a few transportation tips that helped me during my trips to Poznań:

Download the Jakdojade App: This handy app helped me navigate the public transportation system like a local. It provides real-time information on buses, trams, and trains, including schedules and ticket options. You can even purchase your ticket directly through the app.

Currency and Payment: In Poznań, most places accept card payments, but it's a good idea to have some Polish zloty on hand, especially for small purchases or transportation tickets. I found it useful to withdraw cash from an ATM at the airport upon arrival. The exchange rate was better than what I had seen back home.

Know Your Ticket Options: If you're planning to use public transportation frequently, I recommend getting a 24-hour ticket for 15 PLN (€3.30) or a week-long ticket for 50 PLN (€11). Single rides are affordable, but if you're going to explore the city thoroughly, the longer-duration tickets offer better value.

By preparing these small details in advance, I found my arrival in Poznań both smooth and enjoyable. And trust me, once you step into this historical city, you'll be glad you spent time planning the logistics.

Chapter 3

Best Time to Visit and How Long to Stay

Choosing the right time to visit Poznań is key to enjoying your trip to the fullest. When I first visited Poznań, I went in mid-July, basking in the warm weather, lively atmosphere, and the beautiful streets packed with outdoor cafés. However, having returned in winter, I've seen how different the city feels depending on the time of year. Each season in Poznań offers its unique charm and experiences, so let's dive into the best time to plan your trip and how long you should stay.

3.1 Weather by Season: When to Plan Your Trip

The weather in Poznań can greatly influence your experience. The city has a temperate climate, with cold winters and warm summers. Let's take a look at each season to help you decide when to visit.

Spring (March to May)

Spring in Poznań is delightful as the city begins to bloom. If you enjoy moderate temperatures, fewer crowds, and blossoming parks, spring is a perfect time.

Temperatures range from 8°C (46°F) in March to around 18°C (64°F) by May. During my spring visit, I spent time at the Palm House (Palmiarnia Poznańska) in Wilson Park, where I could escape the chill and wander through the tropical greenery. The flowers in the city's many parks also start blooming, making it an ideal season for outdoor lovers.

Opening Hours for Palm House:

Monday to Sunday: 9:00 AM – 4:00 PM

Coordinates: 52.3985° N, 16.8943° E

Address: Matejki 18, 60-771 Poznań, Poland

Contact: +48 61 867 51 45

Price range: 8 PLN (€2) entry for adults

Website: palmiarniapoznan.pl

Summer (June to August)

Summer in Poznań is the peak tourist season, and for a good reason. The weather is warm, with average temperatures hovering between 20°C (68°F) and 25°C (77°F). July is the warmest month, and during this time, I loved exploring the Old Market Square (Stary Rynek), with its vibrant street performances, colorful architecture, and bustling cafés. The long daylight hours gave me ample time to enjoy outdoor activities like a boat ride on Malta Lake or cycling around the city. However, be prepared for crowds at popular attractions, as summer is the most favored time for tourists. If you want a more relaxed experience, consider coming in early June or late August, when the crowds have thinned a little.

Fall (September to November)

Autumn in Poznań is breathtaking, with the trees in Citadel Park (Park Cytadela) turning shades of orange and gold. The weather cools down significantly, with temperatures ranging from 15°C (59°F) in September to around 5°C (41°F) in November. While it can be a bit rainy, it's also a time when the city's cultural scene comes to life, with festivals and art exhibitions popping up. If you're not deterred by cooler temperatures, this is one of my favorite times to visit. I once spent a whole afternoon wandering through Citadel Park's gardens and war memorials, enjoying the tranquility of the season.

Coordinates: 52.4243° N, 16.9331° E

Address: Aleja Armii Poznań, 61-626 Poznań, Poland

Price range: Free entry

Winter (December to February)

If you're a fan of the cold and festive holiday spirit, winter in Poznań can be magical. The temperature often drops below freezing, especially in January, but the city's Christmas Markets are worth braving the cold for. Poznań doesn't experience heavy snowfall compared to other parts of Poland, but the frosty air and holiday lights add a certain charm to the Old Market Square. I remember sipping mulled wine (known locally as grzane wino) at one of the market stalls while admiring the twinkling lights and festive decorations.

One thing to note: if you're planning a winter visit, pack warm clothing, including a good coat, gloves, and a hat, because temperatures can drop to around -5°C (23°F), especially at night.

3.2 Annual Events and Festivals Worth Attending

Poznań is a city of culture, and there's always something happening throughout the year. I was lucky enough to visit during some of the city's most exciting festivals. If you're a fan of events that give you a deep dive into local culture, plan your visit around these popular festivals.

St. Martin's Day (November 11)

St. Martin's Day is one of Poznań's biggest celebrations, with parades, street performances, and, of course, the famous St. Martin's Croissant (Rogal świętomarciński). I attended this festival during one of my autumn visits, and the atmosphere was electrifying. You can grab a croissant (or two) from the numerous stalls dotted around the city. These sweet pastries, filled with white poppy seeds, almonds, and raisins, are a must-try when you're in town.

Price of St. Martin's Croissant: 6-10 PLN (€1.30-2.20) per piece

Website: rogalowemuzeum.pl

Malta Festival (June/July)

The Malta Festival is an international theater and arts festival that takes over the city every summer. It's one of the largest cultural events in Poland, and you'll find performances, exhibitions, and interactive installations scattered around Poznań. When I visited during this festival, I attended a few outdoor theater performances in Wolności Square (Plac Wolności), and the creativity on display was incredible.

Opening Hours: Festival events take place throughout the day and evening.

Website: malta-festival.pl

Poznań International Fair (Various Dates)

If you're visiting for business or simply want to experience a more formal event, the Poznań International Fair (Międzynarodowe Targi Poznańskie) hosts trade shows and exhibitions throughout the year. These range from agricultural fairs to tech conferences and more. The complex itself is massive, and I found the architecture of the pavilions worth a look, even if you're not attending an event.

Coordinates: 52.4057° N, 16.9208° E

Address: Głogowska 14, 60-734 Poznań, Poland

Website: mtp.pl

3.3 How Long to Stay: Tailoring Your Trip

Deciding how long to stay in Poznań really depends on your interests and how much you want to explore.

Based on my experiences, here are some recommendations:

Weekend Getaway (2-3 days): If you're short on time, a weekend is enough to see Poznań's highlights, such as the Old Market Square, the Town Hall, and the Imperial Castle. I did this on one of my visits, focusing mainly on the city center, and still managed to see a lot.

Longer Stay (4-6 days): For those who want to dive deeper into Poznań's culture and history, 4-6 days is ideal. You'll have time to visit museums, parks, and perhaps take a day trip to nearby attractions like Rogalin Palace or Kornik Castle. This is what I opted for during my second visit, and it allowed me to enjoy the city at a more relaxed pace.

Cultural Immersion (1 week or more): If you're really keen on getting to know Poznań, staying for a week or longer will give you the chance to explore not only the main sights but also the hidden gems and local neighborhoods. You could even take a day trip to Wolsztyn, known for its steam locomotive depot.

3.4 What to Pack for Each Season

Packing for Poznań depends heavily on the time of year. Based on my own mistakes and learnings, here are a few packing tips:

Spring/Fall: Bring layers, as the weather can change throughout the day. A light jacket, sweaters, and comfortable walking shoes are essential. Don't forget an umbrella, as rain is common in these seasons.

Summer: Light, breathable clothing will be your best friend in the warmer months. I spent most of my summer trip in shorts and t-shirts, with a light jacket for cooler evenings. Sunscreen and sunglasses are also must-haves.

Winter: Pack warmly! A heavy coat, scarves, gloves, and a hat are essential, as the cold can be biting. I also recommend waterproof boots if you plan on walking a lot, as the streets can get slushy with snow and ice.

Chapter 4

Getting Around Poznań – Transportation

Once you've arrived in Poznań, getting around is a breeze. On my first visit, I was surprised by how well-connected and easy the city is to navigate. Whether you're a fan of public transportation, prefer taxis or ride-sharing apps, or even like to explore on foot, Poznań has plenty of options. Let me guide you through the various ways to get around this charming city, along with some practical tips that made my stay hassle-free.

4.1 Public Transportation: Buses, Trams, and Metro

Public transportation in Poznań is efficient and inexpensive, and the network of buses and trams is extensive, covering the entire city and its surrounding areas. The first thing I did when I arrived was grab a Pekka Card (Poznań City Card), which I highly recommend. It not only gives you unlimited access to public transport but also discounts on attractions and restaurants. You can pick one up at the airport, main train station, or tourist information points around the city.

Trams

Trams are the backbone of Poznań's public transport system, and they are an excellent way to explore the city. There are 22 tram lines in total, operating from 5:00 AM until midnight. The trams are modern and clean, and I found them very easy to use. Some of the most scenic routes run through the Old Town (Stare Miasto), which allows you to sightsee while you travel.

One memorable route I took was Tram No. 5, which goes from the city center to Malta Lake. It's a great way to get to one of Poznań's most popular outdoor spots, where you can enjoy a walk or bike ride around the lake.

Buses

The bus network complements the tram system, especially in areas not covered by the trams. There are numerous day and night bus lines, with buses running frequently during the day and less often during the night. I used Bus No. 52 to get from the city center to the Poznań Zoo, which is located in a more suburban area.

Ticketing and Prices

You can buy tickets at vending machines located at most tram and bus stops, or use the Jakdojade mobile app, which was a lifesaver for me. Tickets are time-based, with options for 15-minute rides (4 PLN), 45-minute rides (6 PLN), and 24-hour tickets (15 PLN). I opted for a 72-hour ticket during my first stay, which cost me 40 PLN (€8.80). Remember to validate your ticket once you board the tram or bus by inserting it into one of the machines.

Opening hours: Trams and buses run from 5:00 AM to midnight.

Price range: Tickets range from 4 PLN (€0.88) for a 15-minute ride to 40 PLN (€8.80) for a 72-hour ticket.

Website: poznan.pl/mim/public_transport

4.2 Taxis, Uber, and Ride-Share Apps

While public transport is efficient, sometimes you just need the convenience of a taxi or ride-share service. On my last trip, I took an Uber from the airport to my hotel, and it was quick and affordable. The Uber app works well in Poznań, and you can also use Bolt, which is another popular ride-share option.

Taxis

If you prefer traditional taxis, they're easy to find at taxi stands throughout the city, especially near train stations, airports, and popular tourist spots like the Old Market Square. I would recommend using registered taxis with meters, as there are a few unregistered taxis that might try to overcharge. The average fare within the city center ranges from 20 PLN to 40 PLN (€4.40 to €8.80), depending on the distance and traffic.

Taxis can also be hailed through popular apps like mytaxi (now FreeNow), which I found convenient as it allows you to book and pay directly through the app, avoiding any cash transactions.

Contact: FreeNow app: +48 22 389 62 80

Price range: Around 20-40 PLN (€4.40-€8.80) for trips within the city.

4.3 Renting a Car or Bicycle

If you prefer the freedom of having your own vehicle or want to explore the countryside around Poznań, renting a car is a great option. During my second trip, I rented a car for a day trip to Rogalin Palace and

Kórnik Castle, and the drive was straightforward, with well-maintained roads and clear signage.

Car Rental

You can rent a car at Poznań-Ławica Airport or from rental agencies in the city. Most international brands like Avis, Hertz, and Sixt are available. The cost of a rental car varies, but you can expect to pay around 100-150 PLN (€22-33) per day for a basic compact car. Keep in mind that parking in the city center can be tricky and expensive, so I would recommend using public transport if you plan to stay within the city limits.

Opening hours: Most car rental agencies operate from 8:00 AM to 8:00 PM.

Price range: 100-150 PLN (€22-33) per day for a compact car.

Renting a Bicycle

For a more eco-friendly and enjoyable way to explore the city, consider renting a bicycle. Poznań has a city bike system called Poznań Bike (Nextbike), with over 100 stations where you can rent a bike and drop it off at any other station. This was my preferred way of exploring the parks and quieter neighborhoods. I rode a bike along the paths by Cytadela Park and around Malta Lake, both of which offer scenic routes.

Renting a bike is cheap and easy. You simply register through the Nextbike app or at a station kiosk, and the first 20 minutes are free. After that, it's 2 PLN (€0.44) for each additional 30 minutes.

Opening hours: 24/7 for the bike-sharing system.

Price range: 2 PLN (€0.44) per 30 minutes after the first 20 minutes.

Website: poznan.pl/mim/public_transport

4.4 Walking Tours: Exploring Poznań on Foot

Walking is one of the best ways to experience Poznań. The city center is compact, and many of its attractions are within walking distance of each other. I loved wandering through the Old Market Square, admiring the colorful facades of the historic townhouses and the famous Town Hall (Ratusz). Every day at noon, the mechanical goats on the Town Hall clock butt heads, which is a must-see for visitors.

Walking tours are also a great way to learn more about the city's history. On one of my visits, I joined a free walking tour that started at Freedom Square (Plac

Wolności) and ended at Ostrów Tumski (Cathedral Island), one of the oldest parts of the city. The guide was knowledgeable and passionate about the city's history, and the tour gave me a deeper appreciation for Poznań's heritage.

While I explored most of the city on foot, I would recommend wearing comfortable shoes, as some of the streets in the Old Town are cobblestoned and can be uneven.

Opening hours: Walking tours usually run twice a day, at 11:00 AM and 3:00 PM.

Price range: Free, but tips are encouraged (I usually gave around 20 PLN (€4.40)).

4.5 Navigating the City: Maps and Local Advice

To navigate Poznań easily, I relied heavily on both physical maps and mobile apps. The city offers plenty of tourist maps, available at the airport, train station, or tourist information centers. I always kept a paper map handy, especially when exploring quieter neighborhoods or venturing outside the city center.

The Jakdojade app, which I mentioned earlier, was indispensable for figuring out tram and bus routes, while Google Maps worked perfectly for walking directions and finding nearby attractions.

A handy local tip I received was to always check for construction updates or tram line changes, as these can happen quite frequently, especially during the summer months. The locals were very helpful, and don't hesitate to ask for directions — many people speak English, particularly in tourist areas.

Chapter 5

Top Tourist Attractions in Poznań

Poznań, a vibrant city nestled in western Poland, holds a special place in my heart. It's a place where history, culture, and modern life harmoniously blend to create an unforgettable travel experience. The first time I arrived in Poznań, I was struck by its charm and the warmth of its people. I wandered through its colorful streets, tasted local delicacies, and explored its historical landmarks. What stood out most were the unique attractions and the stories behind them. Let me walk you through the gems of this magnificent city, one landmark at a time.

5.1 Stary Rynek (Old Market Square)

Stary Rynek, or Old Market Square, is the heart of Poznań, and it's where I started my journey. The square is framed by charming, pastel-colored buildings that date back to the Renaissance, giving the entire place a fairy-tale-like atmosphere. Walking through the cobblestone streets, I felt transported to another era. The square buzzes with life, filled with street performers, locals, and tourists alike.

Opening/Closing Hours: Always open

Coordinates: 52.4083° N, 16.9340° E

Address Contact: Stary Rynek, Poznań, Poland

Price Range: Free to explore

In the summer months, the square transforms into an open-air dining room, with outdoor cafés offering everything from local Polish dishes to international cuisine. I spent an afternoon here savoring a bowl of żurek, a traditional Polish sour rye soup, as I watched the world go by. The square is also home to many festivals and events throughout the year, so there's always something happening.

5.2 Poznań Town Hall and the Famous Goats

Right in the center of Stary Rynek stands the majestic Poznań Town Hall (Ratusz). Built in the 16th century, this Renaissance masterpiece is not only beautiful to look at but also home to one of Poznań's most beloved traditions. Every day at noon, crowds gather to witness the famous mechanical goats emerge from the clock tower and butt heads 12 times. It's an adorable spectacle that draws visitors of all ages.

Opening/Closing Hours: 10:00 AM - 4:00 PM (Closed Mondays)

Coordinates: 52.4083° N, 16.9340° E

Address Contact: Stary Rynek 1, Poznań, Poland

Phone Number: +48 61 856 81 00

Price Range: Free to watch the goats; Town Hall Museum entrance around 8 PLN

I still remember standing with the crowd on a sunny afternoon, eagerly awaiting the goats. The whole square seemed to pause for those few moments, and I couldn't help but smile as the little creatures came to life. The Town Hall also houses a museum, which offers a fascinating glimpse into the history of the city.

5.3 The Imperial Castle

The Imperial Castle (Zamek Cesarski), built for Kaiser Wilhelm II in the early 20th century, is one of the last monarchic castles built in Europe. It has a striking neo-Romanesque design and is steeped in history, having been used for various purposes over the years, including as Nazi headquarters during World War II.

Opening/Closing Hours: 10:00 AM - 5:00 PM

Coordinates: 52.4083° N, 16.9220° E

Address Contact: Święty Marcin 80/82, Poznań, Poland

Phone Number: +48 61 852 03 90

Price Range: Free entry to the castle; guided tours around 20 PLN

What struck me most about this place wasn't just its imposing architecture but its peaceful atmosphere. Inside, there's a stunning chapel and an art gallery. I spent an entire afternoon wandering through its halls, imagining what life must have been like when it was a royal residence.

5.4 Poznań Cathedral and Ostrow Tumski (Cathedral Island)

A short walk from the bustling city center is Ostrow Tumski, or Cathedral Island, the oldest part of Poznań. At its heart stands the magnificent Poznań Cathedral, one of the oldest churches in Poland, dating back to the 10th century.

Opening/Closing Hours: 9:00 AM - 6:00 PM

Coordinates: 52.4112° N, 16.9485° E

Address Contact: Ostrów Tumski 17, Poznań, Poland

Phone Number: +48 61 852 96 05

Price Range: Free entry; guided tours around 15 PLN

Walking along the Warta River and onto the island, I felt a sense of peace. The cathedral's Gothic towers rise above the skyline, and its interior is equally impressive, with intricate stained glass and the tombs of Poland's first rulers. I joined a guided tour that delved deep into the history of the island and the early days of Poland's Christianization.

5.5 Malta Lake and Its Outdoor Activities

For a more modern escape, Malta Lake (Jezioro Maltańskie) is a great place to unwind. Located just a few kilometers east of the city center, this man-made lake is surrounded by green spaces, bike paths, and even a ski slope! I rented a bike and rode around the lake, stopping for a picnic by the water.

Opening/Closing Hours: Always open

Coordinates: 52.4008° N, 16.9760° E

Address Contact: Malta Lake, Poznań, Poland

Price Range: Free to visit; various activities priced individually (e.g., ski slope around 40 PLN for a day pass)

In the summer, the lake is popular for boating and kayaking, while in the winter, locals and tourists alike hit the slopes at the Malta Ski Resort. If you're feeling adventurous, there's even an alpine coaster that zooms through the hills by the lake!

5.6 Citadel Park and War Memorials

Citadel Park (Park Cytadela) is Poznań's largest park, and it's filled with historical monuments, war memorials, and lush greenery. It's the perfect place to escape the city's hustle and bustle. As I strolled through the park, I came across the Poznań Army Museum and several war memorials, including the impressive monument to the heroes of the Polish Army.

Opening/Closing Hours: Always open

Coordinates: 52.4225° N, 16.9372° E

Address Contact: Aleja Armii Poznań, Poznań, Poland

Price Range: Free entry; museum entry around 10 PLN

This park is a beautiful tribute to Poznań's history, and it offers plenty of peaceful spots to relax or have a picnic. I spent hours here, exploring the trails and soaking in the city's past.

5.7 Croissant Museum and Poznań's Legendary Rogal świętomarciński

No visit to Poznań is complete without tasting the famous Rogal świętomarciński—a delicious croissant filled with poppy seeds and nuts. At the Croissant Museum, not only did I get to sample this tasty treat, but I also learned how it's made. The museum offers interactive baking demonstrations, where you can try your hand at making your own croissant.

Opening/Closing Hours: 10:00 AM - 6:00 PM

Coordinates: 52.4083° N, 16.9340° E

Address Contact: Stary Rynek 41, Poznań, Poland

Phone Number: +48 61 307 13 13

Price Range: Entry around 12 PLN

Watching the locals bake these traditional pastries was a fun experience, and it made me appreciate the history and craftsmanship behind each Rogal świętomarciński. I couldn't leave without buying a few to enjoy later!

5.8 National Museum of Poznań

The National Museum of Poznań (Muzeum Narodowe w Poznaniu) is a treasure trove of Polish and European art. The museum's collection ranges from medieval art to contemporary works, and there's something for every art lover to enjoy.

Opening/Closing Hours: 9:00 AM - 5:00 PM (Closed on Mondays)

Coordinates: 52.4080° N, 16.9285° E

Address Contact: Al. Marcinkowskiego 9, Poznań, Poland

Phone Number: +48 61 856 80 00

Price Range: Entry around 20 PLN

I spent an afternoon wandering through the galleries, captivated by the beautiful paintings and sculptures. The museum's highlight is its impressive collection of

Polish art, but there are also works by famous European artists like Claude Monet.

5.9 Palmiarnia (Palm House) in Wilson Park

Located in Wilson Park, the Poznań Palm House (Palmiarnia Poznańska) is one of the largest botanical gardens in Europe. With over 17,000 species of plants from all over the world, it's a lush, tropical escape in the heart of the city.

Opening/Closing Hours: 9:00 AM - 5:00 PM (Closed on Mondays)

Coordinates: 52.3989° N, 16.9083° E

Address Contact: Matejki 18, Poznań, Poland

Phone Number: +48 61 866 40 48

Price Range: Entry around 12 PLN

I loved wandering through the various rooms, each with its unique climate and ecosystem. There's even a small aquarium in the Palm House, making it a great spot for families with children.

5.10 Poznań's Fara Church

Last but not least, Poznań's Fara Church (Bazylika Kolegiacka Matki Bożej Nieustającej Pomocy) is a Baroque masterpiece that took my breath away the moment I stepped inside. Its lavish interior, adorned with gold and marble, is truly a sight to behold.

Opening/Closing Hours: 9:00 AM - 6:00 PM

Coordinates: 52.4076° N, 16.9335° E

Address Contact: Gołębia 1, Poznań, Poland

Phone Number: +48 61 852 69 80

Price Range: Free entry

I visited during a quiet weekday afternoon, and the peaceful atmosphere inside the church was a stark contrast to the busy streets outside. It's the perfect place to reflect and admire the artistry of the Baroque period.

Chapter 6

What to Do (and What Not to Do) in Poznań

After exploring the top tourist attractions, I quickly realized that Poznań has much more to offer than just beautiful sights. There are unique experiences to try, cultural norms to respect, and ways to avoid common tourist pitfalls. Here's what I learned during my time in this remarkable city.

6.1 Must-Try Experiences in Poznań

One of the best experiences in Poznań is, without a doubt, trying Rogal świętomarciński at the Croissant Museum. I also highly recommend renting a bike and riding around Malta Lake. The bike paths are well-maintained, and the lake offers stunning views, especially at sunset.

For history buffs, a visit to Ostrow Tumski and Poznań's cathedral is a must. The guided tour I took was incredibly informative and gave me a deeper understanding of the city's roots. Lastly, if you're an art lover like me, don't miss the National Museum—its diverse collection will keep you captivated for hours.

6.2 Cultural Etiquette and Local Norms

Polish people are generally warm and welcoming, but it's important to observe certain cultural norms. Poles are quite punctual, so if you've made plans with locals, be sure to arrive on time. I also noticed that people are quite formal in their greetings, especially when meeting for the first time. A polite "Dzień dobry" (Good day) or "Cześć" (Hi) will go a long way in making a good first impression.

6.3 Do's and Don'ts for a Respectful Visit

Do respect the local customs and dress modestly when visiting churches and religious sites.

Don't forget to tip at restaurants and cafés—around 10% is customary.

Do try to learn a few basic Polish phrases; locals will appreciate the effort.

Don't be loud or disruptive in public places, especially on public transport.

During my stay, I found that a little effort to respect these norms made my interactions with locals much more pleasant.

6.4 How to Avoid Tourist Traps

While Poznań isn't as overrun with tourists as some other European cities, there are still a few places where you should be cautious. I noticed that some restaurants around Stary Rynek can be overpriced, catering primarily to tourists. Instead, I recommend venturing a little further from the main square to find more authentic and reasonably priced Polish food.

Another tip is to book your tours and activities in advance. I was able to get a better price for my Malta Ski Resort ticket by booking online rather than purchasing it at the gate.

6.5 Safety Tips for a Hassle-Free Stay

Poznań is a relatively safe city, but like any travel destination, it's always good to stay vigilant. Here are some safety tips I followed during my trip:

Keep your belongings close in crowded areas, especially around Stary Rynek.

Use licensed taxis or ride-sharing apps like Bolt or Uber if you need to get around late at night.

Stick to well-lit, populated areas when walking at night.

During my stay, I felt completely safe, even when wandering around late at night. The city has a friendly vibe, and as long as you take common-sense precautions, you'll have a worry-free experience.

Looking back on my time in Poznań, I can say that it was one of the most enriching and enjoyable trips I've ever taken. The mix of history, culture, and modernity, along with the warmth of the people, made it a destination I'll never forget. Whether you're marveling at the Town Hall goats, savoring a Rogal świętomarciński, or relaxing by Malta Lake, there's something here for everyone. If you haven't been yet, I can't recommend it enough.

Chapter 7

Accommodation – Where to Stay

When I first visited Poznań, finding the right place to stay was a big part of the adventure. Poznań offers a variety of accommodation options, from luxurious hotels with views over the Old Market Square to cozy boutique guesthouses tucked away in quieter parts of the city. I stayed in a range of places during my time here, and I want to share the best options, depending on what you're looking for.

A. Overview of Accommodation Options

No matter your budget or taste, Poznań has something for everyone. You can choose from high-end luxury hotels, affordable but charming budget options, and even some uniquely historical stays. Many visitors gravitate towards staying near the Old Town, which is central and offers proximity to many attractions, but there are also quieter neighborhoods with local character. You could find a place that feels like home for a few days or even weeks.

B. Luxury Resorts

For those who want to indulge in luxury, Poznań has a few standout options that will make you feel pampered. The Sheraton Poznań Hotel, located at Bukowska 3/9 (52.4064° N, 16.9111° E), is a fantastic choice. I spent a weekend there, and I can tell you the service was impeccable, and the spa was a perfect way to unwind after a day of exploring.

Address: Bukowska 3/9, 60-809 Poznań

Contact: +48 61 655 2000

Price Range: 450–800 PLN per night

Website: sheratonpoznan.pl

Another favorite for those seeking an elegant experience is the Hotel Blow Up Hall 5050, famous for its modern, artistic flair and chic rooms. It's located inside the historic Stary Browar shopping center, so shopping and dining are literally at your doorstep.

Address: Kościuszki 42, 61-891 Poznań

Contact: +48 61 657 9090

Price Range: 600–1,200 PLN per night

Website: blowuphall5050.pl

C. Budget-Friendly Hotels

When I traveled on a tighter budget, I found some real gems. Hotel Ibis Poznań Stare Miasto is a perfect example of affordable comfort. The rooms are clean and modern, and the hotel is just a 10-minute walk from the Old Market Square, which made it incredibly convenient. It's located at Kazimierza Wielkiego 23 (52.4035° N, 16.9387° E).

Address: Kazimierza Wielkiego 23, 61-863 Poznań

Contact: +48 61 858 4400

Price Range: 150–250 PLN per night

Website: ibis.com

Another great budget option is Traffic Hotel, located close to the Poznań International Fair and the main train station, so it's easy to explore the city from here.

Address: Niezłomnych 1C, 61-894 Poznań

Contact: +48 61 833 5546

Price Range: 120–200 PLN per night

Website: traffic-hotel.pl

D. Boutique Guesthouses

One of my favorite stays in Poznań was at a boutique guesthouse. The Garden Boutique Residence, just a stone's throw from the Old Town Square, offers charming, individually decorated rooms in a historic building. It feels like staying in a friend's stylish home, rather than a hotel.

Address: Wroniecka 24, 61-763 Poznań

Contact: +48 61 852 6264

Price Range: 250–400 PLN per night

Website: gardenboutique.pl

Another quaint option is Rosemary's Hostel, which has a cozy and artsy atmosphere that makes it feel far more personal than a typical budget hotel.

Address: Gwarna 13, 60-703 Poznań

Contact: +48 601 305 062

Price Range: 60–150 PLN per night

Website: rosemaryhostel.pl

E. Unique Stays: Apartments and Historic Buildings

If you're looking for a unique stay, Poznań has several options for short-term apartment rentals and historic buildings converted into accommodation. I rented an apartment via Stay99 Apartments, located right in the Old Market Square, and it gave me a true taste of life in the heart of Poznań.

Address: Wielka 23, 61-774 Poznań

Contact: +48 500 018 002

Price Range: 200–500 PLN per night

Website: stay99.pl

For something more historic, check out Apartamenty Pomarańczarnia on Rybaki Street, which is housed in a beautifully renovated 19th-century building.

Address: Rybaki 12, 61-883 Poznań

Contact: +48 61 851 5143

Price Range: 180–350 PLN per night

Website: pomaranczarnia.com.pl

F. Top Recommended Accommodation

In terms of overall recommendations, I'd say Sheraton Poznań for luxury, Hotel Ibis Stare Miasto for budget-conscious travelers, and Garden Boutique Residence for those who want a boutique experience. These options cover the spectrum of price and style, ensuring there's something for everyone.

G. Choosing the Right Accommodation for You

When choosing where to stay, consider the purpose of your trip. Are you here for business or leisure? Do you want to be close to the hustle and bustle of the Old Town, or do you prefer a quieter spot? For business travelers, staying near Poznań International Fair might make sense, while tourists may prefer accommodations near the Old Market Square or Malta Lake for convenience and easy access to the city's main attractions.

H. Booking Tips and Tricks

From my experience, booking ahead, especially during peak seasons like summer or around Christmas markets, is essential. I found that many places offer significant discounts for early bookings, especially apartments. If you're looking for last-minute deals, apps like Booking.com or Airbnb have good options, but don't forget to check directly with the hotel or apartment for even better rates.

Chapter 8

Where and What to Eat – A Culinary Journey

One of the highlights of visiting Poznań is diving into its food scene. The city has a rich culinary tradition, and trying the local dishes is a must. From the famous St. Martin's Croissants to hearty pierogi, there's something to satisfy every palate. During my time in the city, I had some of the best meals of my life, and I'll share my favorite spots and experiences with you.

8.1 Must-Try Traditional Dishes

You can't visit Poznań without trying Rogal świętomarciński (St. Martin's Croissants). These crescent-shaped pastries are filled with a sweet, white poppy seed filling, and they are simply heavenly. The best place to get them is from Cukiernia Kandulski, a bakery renowned for its croissants.

Address: Plac Wolności 6, 61-738 Poznań

Contact: +48 61 852 3186

Price Range: 10–15 PLN per croissant

Website: cukierniakandulski.pl

Another must-try is pyry z gzikiem, a traditional dish of potatoes served with cottage cheese and cream. It's simple but delicious and can be found at Pod Niebieniem in the Old Town.

Address: Stary Rynek 64/65, 61-772 Poznań

Contact: +48 61 855 0353

Price Range: 25–35 PLN per dish

Website: podniebieniem.pl

8.2 Poznań's Best Restaurants and Cafés

Poznań has a vibrant restaurant scene, and I found that there's something for every taste and budget. For a special evening, I recommend Restauracja Muga. It's a fine-dining restaurant where the chef creates modern takes on Polish classics. The attention to detail here is impeccable.

Address: ul. Krysiewicza 5, 61-825 Poznań

Contact: +48 61 222 3161

Price Range: 100–300 PLN per meal

Website: restauracjamuga.pl

For a more casual, but equally delicious meal, head to Pierogarnia Stary Młyn. This cozy spot serves up a wide variety of pierogi (Polish dumplings), both savory and sweet. My favorite was the pierogi stuffed with wild mushrooms and cream.

Address: Stary Rynek 52, 61-772 Poznań

Contact: +48 61 852 8303

Price Range: 20–50 PLN per meal

Website: pierogarniastarymlyn.pl

8.3 Street Food and Quick Eats

If you're in a hurry, don't miss the food trucks scattered around the city. I stumbled upon a fantastic truck serving zapiekanka (a Polish-style baguette with melted cheese and toppings) near Plac Wolności. It's perfect for a quick, satisfying snack.

Location: Plac Wolności (52.4093° N, 16.9335° E)

Price Range: 10–20 PLN

Another quick bite that's become a favorite of mine is Kebab Poznań, a local institution. They serve some of the best kebabs I've had outside the Middle East.

Address: Garbary 42, 61-869 Poznań

Contact: +48 61 852 6744

Price Range: 15–25 PLN per kebab

Website: kebabpoznan.pl

8.4 Vegan and Vegetarian Options

Poznań has embraced the plant-based trend, and there are several great spots for vegan and vegetarian food. One of the best is Wypas, a fully vegan restaurant with creative dishes that even non-vegans will love. I had the vegan pierogi there, and they were fantastic.

Address: Jackowskiego 38, 60-508 Poznań

Contact: +48 603 112 884

Price Range: 30–50 PLN per meal

Website: wypas.pl

Another good option is Kwadrat, a casual vegan bistro with a focus on fresh, healthy ingredients. It's a great place to stop for lunch while exploring the city.

Address: Kościuszki 68, 61-891 Poznań

Contact: +48 61 848 6074

Price Range: 20–40 PLN per meal

Website: kwadratbistro.pl

8.5 Dining Etiquette and Local Customs

Dining in Poznań is generally casual, but it's good to know a few local customs. For example, tipping is expected at most restaurants, with 10-15% being the standard. When you enter a restaurant, it's common to wait to be seated rather than seating yourself. I also noticed that meals tend to be more leisurely than in other parts of Europe, so take your time and enjoy the experience.

8.6 Food Tours: Exploring Poznań's Culinary Scene

One of the best ways to experience Poznań's food scene is by joining a food tour. I went on one with Eat Polska, and it was a fantastic way to sample a variety of dishes and learn about the history and culture behind them.

Price Range: 200–300 PLN per person

Website: eatpolska.com

The tour took us to several spots, including a bakery for St. Martin's Croissants, a pierogi restaurant, and even a bar for some local craft beers. By the end of the tour, I felt like I had a true taste of Poznań.

I hope this guide gives you a well-rounded sense of the amazing accommodation and dining options available in Poznań. Whether you're traveling on a budget, looking for luxury, or wanting to immerse yourself in the local culture, this city has so much to offer. Don't forget to enjoy every bite and every stay, just as I did!

Chapter 9

Itineraries for Every Traveler

A. Weekend Getaway: Exploring the Essentials

I remember the first time I arrived in Poznań on a Friday evening. It was late summer, and the Old Town was buzzing with life. My first stop had to be the Stary Rynek, the central square. As I strolled through the cobbled streets, I couldn't help but be enchanted by the colorful merchant houses surrounding the square. The Renaissance-style Poznań Town Hall, with its iconic clock featuring two mechanical goats, stands as the focal point. It's a tradition to watch them butt heads at noon each day, a quirky sight you shouldn't miss.

The Royal-Imperial Route (Trakt Królewsko-Cesarski) is a must for any weekend traveler. It's a walking tour that traces the history of the city from its medieval roots to its modern incarnation. The route also takes you past Ostrów Tumski (Cathedral Island), home to the oldest cathedral in Poland, Poznań Cathedral. Make sure to visit the Archaeological Reserve Genius Loci for a deeper dive into Poznań's ancient history.

Opening hours: Stary Rynek: Always open

Coordinates: 52.4085° N, 16.9344° E

Address: Stary Rynek, Poznań, Poland

Price range: Free entry for the Old Town, small fees for museums on Cathedral Island.

B. Cultural Immersion: Museums, Art, and History

When I wanted to dive deeper into Poznań's culture, I spent a full day exploring its museums and historical sites. My favorite? The National Museum in Poznań (Muzeum Narodowe w Poznaniu). It houses an impressive collection of Polish and European art, including works by famous artists like Jacek Malczewski and Jan Matejko. I remember standing in front of The Polish Rider painting, lost in its vivid imagery.

Don't skip the Rogal Museum (Museum of Croissants), where you can participate in a demonstration of how to make Poznań's famous Rogal Świętomarciński, a delicious pastry traditionally baked for St. Martin's Day. The storytelling by the museum staff is as rich as the filling in those croissants!

Opening hours: National Museum: 9 AM to 5 PM, closed on Mondays

Coordinates: 52.4090° N, 16.9293° E

Address: Al. Marcinkowskiego 9, 61-745 Poznań, Poland

Phone number: +48 61 856 80 00

Price range: Around 20 PLN for the National Museum, 19 PLN for the Rogal Museum.

Website Address: muzeumnarodowe.poznan.pl

C. Outdoor Adventure: Nature and Activity-Filled Days

Poznań is also a fantastic destination for outdoor lovers. I spent a morning cycling around Lake Malta, a large artificial lake east of the city center. There's something incredibly calming about the combination of water, greenery, and fresh air. The area is filled with activities, including a ski slope, mini-golf, and the New Zoo, which is a great spot for a relaxing stroll among animals. I rented a paddleboat for an hour, just to soak in the peaceful surroundings.

Another great place to visit is the Citadel Park (Park Cytadela), Poznań's largest park. It's a mix of history and nature, with remnants of military fortifications scattered throughout. I spent hours wandering the park's vast trails, pausing at the Museum of Armament to check out their outdoor exhibition of tanks and aircraft.

Opening hours: Lake Malta: Always open, Zoo: 9 AM to 7 PM

Coordinates: Lake Malta: 52.4080° N, 16.9821° E

Address: Lake Malta, Poznań, Poland

Phone number: +48 61 877 90 30

Price range: Free entry to parks, zoo tickets around 30 PLN for adults

Website Address: zoo.poznan.pl

D. Family-Friendly Trip: Fun for All Ages

I brought my nieces to Poznań once, and it was one of the best family trips I've had. The kids adored the New Zoo at Lake Malta, especially the elephants and the miniature train that loops around the zoo. We also spent time at Jump Arena, an indoor trampoline park, which was an absolute hit for burning off some energy.

For a more educational stop, we visited the Brama Poznania Interactive Heritage Center. It's an engaging multimedia experience that walks visitors through the history of Poznań and the beginnings of Polish Christianity. It's incredibly interactive, and even the younger ones were fascinated by the storytelling.

Opening hours: Brama Poznania: 9 AM to 6 PM

Coordinates: 52.4086° N, 16.9484° E

Address: Gdańska 2, 61-123 Poznań, Poland

Phone number: +48 61 647 76 34

Price range: Brama Poznania: 25 PLN per person

Website Address: bramapoznania.pl

E. Budget Travel: How to Make the Most on a Budget

Poznań is an affordable destination compared to many European cities. During my budget trip, I stayed at a cozy hostel in Jeżyce, one of the trendiest areas of the city. Explorer Hostel was a steal for just 50 PLN per night.

Eating on a budget was also easy. I often grabbed zapiekanka (a Polish-style pizza bread) from street vendors for about 8 PLN. For a traditional Polish meal without breaking the bank, I visited Pyra Bar, a quirky restaurant where every dish revolves around potatoes. A filling meal there set me back around 15 PLN.

For free activities, you can easily spend a day wandering around Ostrów Tumski, or exploring the free exhibitions at Galeria Miejska Arsenał.

Coordinates: Explorer Hostel: 52.4069° N, 16.9202° E

Address: Ul. Dąbrowskiego 27A, 60-842 Poznań, Poland

Phone number: +48 61 853 30 70

Price range: 50 PLN for a hostel bed

Website Address: explorerhostel.pl

F. Solo Traveler's Guide: Exploring Poznań Independently

As a solo traveler, Poznań felt incredibly safe and welcoming. I started my solo journey at the Old Brewery Shopping, Arts, and Business Center (Stary Browar). It's an award-winning blend of art gallery, shopping mall, and public space. I loved the mix of modern art installations and high-end shops.

One of my most peaceful moments was spending a solo afternoon in Park Wilsona, a beautifully landscaped park with a large palm house (Palmiarnia Poznańska). Sitting there with a book in hand, surrounded by exotic plants, was a delightful escape from the city's buzz.

Opening hours: Palmiarnia Poznańska: 9 AM to 4 PM, closed on Mondays

Coordinates: 52.3939° N, 16.9007° E

Address: Park Wilsona, Poznań, Poland

Phone number: +48 61 866 40 30

Price range: 10 PLN for the palm house

Website Address: palmiarnia.poznan.pl

G. Romantic Getaways: Couple's Escape

When I planned a romantic weekend with my partner, Poznań surprised me with its romantic charm. We booked a room at Blow Up Hall 5050, an art-hotel within the Stary Browar shopping and arts center. The hotel's minimalist, artsy vibe made it feel luxurious and intimate.

For dinner, we headed to Restauracja Toga near the Old Town, known for its intimate atmosphere and refined Polish cuisine. Afterward, we strolled hand-in-hand through the Citadel Park, which is even more magical during sunset.

Coordinates: Blow Up Hall 5050: 52.4025° N, 16.9256° E

Address: Ul. Kościuszki 42, 61-891 Poznań, Poland

Phone number: +48 61 657 91 00

Price range: Rooms from 400 PLN per night

Website Address: blowuphall.com

Chapter 10

Poznań's Cultural Scene

10.1 Museums and Art Galleries

As a culture enthusiast, I found Poznań to be a haven for museum-goers and art lovers. The National Museum has already been mentioned, but there's also Galeria Miejska Arsenał, which focuses on contemporary art. I stumbled upon this gallery while wandering the Old Town and was intrigued by its ever-changing exhibitions, showcasing both Polish and international artists.

10.2 Theater and Live Performances

During my last visit, I attended a play at the Teatr Wielki (Grand Theatre), a historic opera house. The building itself is stunning, with its neoclassical architecture. It felt like stepping into another era as I watched a performance of Carmen. Tickets were affordable, and I would recommend this experience to anyone who appreciates theater.

Opening hours: Performances typically start at 7 PM

Coordinates: 52.4093° N, 16.9182° E

Address: Ul. Fredry 9, 61-701 Poznań, Poland

Phone number: +48 61 659 02 80

Price range: Tickets from 50 PLN

Website Address: operapoznan.pl

10.3 Film Festivals and Cinemas

Poznań also hosts the Ale Kino! International Young Audience Film Festival, one of the oldest children's film festivals in Europe. I attended a screening at Kino Muza, an arthouse cinema. The vintage vibe of this small cinema made the experience even more special.

Opening hours: Varies with screenings

Coordinates: 52.4060° N, 16.9254° E

Address: Ul. Św. Marcin 30, 61-806 Poznań, Poland

Phone number: +48 61 852 34 03

Price range: Tickets from 20 PLN

Website Address: kinomuza.pl

10.4 Music and Concerts: Classical to Contemporary

Poznań's music scene is diverse, and I've had the chance to attend both classical and contemporary concerts. The Poznań Philharmonic is renowned for its classical performances, and I once enjoyed an unforgettable evening there, listening to the works of Chopin. For more modern tastes, the Tama Club is a great venue for electronic and indie music.

Opening hours: Concerts typically start at 8 PM

Coordinates: Poznań Philharmonic: 52.4088° N, 16.9220° E

Address: Al. Niepodległości 53, 61-714 Poznań, Poland

Phone number: +48 61 852 47 08

Price range: Tickets from 40 PLN

Website Address: filharmoniapoznanska.pl

10.5 Poznań's Street Art and Public Installations

I was pleasantly surprised by Poznań's thriving street art scene. Jeżyce, the district where I stayed, is filled with vibrant murals. One of the most famous is the Pociąg mural, a massive depiction of a train that stretches across several buildings. It's easy to miss if you're not looking for it, but discovering it feels like finding a hidden treasure.

Coordinates: 52.4156° N, 16.9067° E

Address: Ul. Dąbrowskiego 25, 60-838 Poznań, Poland

Price range: Free

In all, Poznań offers a rich blend of history, culture, and modern charm—whether you're there for a weekend or a week.

Chapter 11

Adventure and Outdoor Activities

11.1 Hiking and Nature Trails

When I first arrived in Poznań, I was struck by how green the city is. You don't have to wander far to find beautiful parks, trails, and areas perfect for hiking. One of my favorite experiences was hiking around Citadel Park (Park Cytadela). This massive park, located at 52.4210° N, 16.9315° E, is the largest park in Poznań and offers a peaceful escape from the bustling city. The park is not only an oasis of green but also filled with historical monuments, including war memorials and military exhibits. As I wandered the trails, I couldn't help but feel connected to the past, knowing that this land was once a fortress and battlefield. It's a perfect place to relax, enjoy nature, and learn a bit of Polish history.

Opening hours: Open 24 hours

Coordinates: 52.4210° N, 16.9315° E

Address: Arcybiskupa Antoniego Baraniaka 1, 61-131 Poznań

Contact: +48 61 852 29 30

Price range: Free

Another trail I explored was at Wielkopolska National Park, about 15 km south of the city, located at 52.2500° N, 16.7500° E. This national park is a haven for outdoor lovers with over 85 km of hiking trails through forests, lakes, and marshlands. The trails are well-marked and cater to all levels of hikers. I personally loved the 5 km Mosiński Trail, which takes you through beautiful wooded areas and along serene lakes. The views were stunning, especially at sunrise when the mist rises from the water, giving the place a mystical atmosphere.

Opening hours: Open 24 hours

Coordinates: 52.2500° N, 16.7500° E

Address: Jeziorna 1, 62-050 Mosina

Contact: +48 61 813 05 51

Price range: Free

11.2 Watersports and Boating on Malta Lake

When the weather heats up in Poznań, Malta Lake (Jezioro Maltańskie) becomes the go-to spot for outdoor enthusiasts. This artificial lake is located at 52.4087° N, 16.9732° E, just a short tram ride from the city center, and offers a range of watersports. I spent a memorable summer afternoon here, renting a kayak and paddling along the calm waters. For about 25 PLN per hour, I got to enjoy the lake from a unique perspective, surrounded by lush greenery. There's also the option for stand-up paddleboarding (SUP), which costs around 40 PLN per hour.

If you're more into speed, there are pedal boats available for rent too. A friend of mine and I rented one for about 35 PLN an hour, and it was the perfect way to relax while taking in the stunning views of the nearby Poznań Ski Slope and Malta's shores.

Opening hours: Typically 8 AM – 8 PM (depending on season)

Coordinates: 52.4087° N, 16.9732° E

Address: ul. Wiankowa 3, 61-131 Poznań

Contact: +48 61 877 54 44

Price range: 25-40 PLN per hour (varies by activity)

11.3 Cycling Routes Around Poznań

Poznań is a fantastic city for cycling, whether you're a casual rider or a more seasoned cyclist. One of the most scenic routes I found runs along the banks of the Warta River, from Chwaliszewo all the way to Starołęka. The trail is flat and easy to navigate, making it perfect for families or those looking to enjoy a relaxed ride. I rented a bike for the day at one of the local shops for about 50 PLN, and the route took me through peaceful riverside views and past several beautiful bridges.

Another excellent cycling route is around Malta Lake, where the trail circles the lake and connects to various other paths. This was one of my favorite spots for an evening ride, particularly at sunset when the light reflects off the water, creating a gorgeous, tranquil scene.

Opening hours: N/A (bike paths are open 24/7)

Coordinates: 52.4087° N, 16.9732° E (Malta Lake area)

Address: Multiple routes around the city

Price range: 50 PLN per day for bike rentals

11.4 Skiing and Winter Sports near Poznań

When winter rolls around, you don't have to travel far from Poznań to enjoy some winter sports. The Malta Ski (Malta-Ski Poznań) is a ski slope located at 52.4053° N, 16.9635° E, right by Malta Lake. Even though it's an artificial slope, it's perfect for beginners and those who want to practice their skiing or snowboarding without heading into the mountains. I had a blast learning the basics here, with a full day of skiing costing around 70 PLN for equipment rental and access to the slope. There's also a 560-meter-long Alpine Coaster ride, which I couldn't resist trying—it's a great thrill, even for adults!

Opening hours: Typically 10 AM – 8 PM (depending on season)

Coordinates: 52.4053° N, 16.9635° E

Address: ul. Wiankowa 2, 61-131 Poznań

Contact: +48 61 876 65 40

Price range: 70 PLN per day for skiing

11.5 Adventure Parks and Ziplining for Thrill-Seekers

If you're an adrenaline junkie like me, Poznań has you covered. The Pyrland Park Linowy is an adventure park located at 52.4300° N, 16.9300° E, just outside Citadel Park. This place is perfect for families or groups of friends looking to challenge themselves with a range of high ropes courses and ziplining. I spent an exhilarating afternoon here, conquering the various courses that range in difficulty. The zipline over the trees was the highlight for me, offering incredible views and a rush of excitement as you soar through the air. Entrance to the park costs around 40 PLN per person, which I found quite reasonable for the level of fun and thrill.

Opening hours: 10 AM – 6 PM

Coordinates: 52.4300° N, 16.9300° E

Address: Aleja Niepodległości 9, 61-714 Poznań

Contact: +48 797 705 455

Price range: 40 PLN per person

Chapter 12

Shopping in Poznań

12.1 Traditional Souvenirs and Local Crafts

When it comes to souvenirs, Poznań has no shortage of unique and beautiful items. One of my favorite places to buy traditional Polish crafts was the Cepelia Shop, located in the Old Market Square at 52.4075° N, 16.9341° E. This shop specializes in handcrafted goods, from colorful pottery to intricate lacework. I picked up a beautiful set of hand-painted ceramics for around 50 PLN, which I still use today for my morning coffee.

Opening hours: 9 AM – 6 PM

Coordinates: 52.4075° N, 16.9341° E

Address: Stary Rynek 10, 61-772 Poznań

Contact: +48 61 852 23 44

Price range: Varies depending on item

12.2 Best Shopping Streets and Markets

Poznań's Święty Marcin Street is one of the best areas for shopping. Located at 52.4093° N, 16.9247° E, this long, bustling street is lined with boutiques, international brands, and local shops. I spent a delightful afternoon wandering along Święty Marcin, popping into stores and picking up a few unique clothing pieces that I couldn't find back home. The street is particularly lively during the Christmas season when it's adorned with festive lights and a holiday market pops up, offering seasonal goods and treats.

For those looking for something more local, the Jeżycki Market is a great place to visit. Located at 52.4181° N, 16.9084° E, this market is filled with fresh produce, local cheeses, flowers, and crafts. It's a perfect place to shop if you're looking to bring home authentic Polish flavors.

Opening hours: Typically 9 AM – 7 PM

Coordinates: 52.4093° N, 16.9247° E (Święty Marcin)

Address: Various locations along Święty Marcin Street and Jeżycki Market

Price range: Varies by store or vendor

12.3 Modern Shopping Malls and Boutiques

Poznań is also home to several modern shopping malls that cater to every need. Stary Browar, located at 52.4046° N, 16.9273° E, is a shopping and art center housed in a former brewery. It's a perfect blend of old and new, with a stunning architectural design and a wide range of high-end stores, as well as a selection of restaurants and cafes. I found a gorgeous handbag here for 300 PLN, and even if you're not in the mood to shop, it's worth visiting for the art exhibitions.

Opening hours: 9 AM – 9 PM

Coordinates: 52.4046° N, 16.9273° E

Address: ul. Półwiejska 32, 61-888 Poznań

Contact: +48 61 859 60 00

Price range: Mid to high-end

12.4 Hidden Gems: Specialty Stores and Artisan Shops

One hidden gem I discovered was the Poznań Coffee Roasters at 52.4042° N, 16.9303° E. As a coffee enthusiast, I couldn't pass up the chance to visit this specialty shop, where they roast their beans in-house. The aroma alone was enough to lure me in, and after trying their coffee, I walked away with a freshly roasted bag for about 40 PLN. It made for a perfect souvenir and brought back memories of my trip every time I brewed a cup back home.

Opening hours: 9 AM – 6 PM

Coordinates: 52.4042° N, 16.9303° E

Address: ul. Świętosławska 7, 61-840 Poznań

Price range: 40 PLN for a bag of coffee

12.5 Where to Buy the Famous St. Martin's Croissant

No trip to Poznań is complete without trying a St. Martin's Croissant (Rogal Świętomarciński), a local delicacy with a rich history. The best place to buy one is from the Poznań Croissant Museum, located at

52.4076° N, 16.9351° E, right in the Old Market Square. The museum not only offers a chance to learn about the croissant's history and how it's made, but you can also purchase one of these sweet treats for around 15 PLN. It's the perfect way to experience a bit of Poznań's culinary heritage.

Opening hours: 10 AM – 6 PM

Coordinates: 52.4076° N, 16.9351° E

Address: ul. Klasztorna 23, 61-772 Poznań

Contact: +48 61 222 74 05

Price range: 15 PLN per croissant

I hope this comprehensive guide helps you experience the best of outdoor activities and shopping in Poznań. My personal adventures in these places made for unforgettable moments, and I know they will do the same for you!

Chapter 13

Nightlife and Entertainment

13.1 Poznań's Top Bars and Clubs

Poznań has a vibrant nightlife scene that kept me on my toes for my entire stay. My first stop was Pijalnia Wódki i Piwa (Taczaka 21, 61-819 Poznań), a nostalgic spot designed like an old communist-era bar. The decor alone was worth the visit, but the real treat was the affordable shots of flavored vodka, starting at around 5 PLN each. The place gets packed quickly, so if you're looking for a lively atmosphere, it's perfect.

Another place that left a lasting impression was Tama (Niezłomnych 2, 61-894 Poznań), a club that hosts techno and electronic music events. The sound system is top-notch, and the underground vibe makes you feel like you're in the heart of a European rave scene. Prices vary by event, with entrance fees usually between 30-50 PLN.

Coordinates: 52.4095° N, 16.9319° E

Opening Hours: Bars typically open around 5 PM and close at 3 AM. Clubs stay open until the early morning hours.

13.2 Where to Enjoy Live Music and Performances

If live music is more your thing, then Blue Note (Kościuszki 79, 61-891 Poznań) is a must-visit. Located in the Zamek Cultural Center, this jazz club gave me one of the best evenings in Poznań. The intimate atmosphere, paired with world-class jazz performances, is a combo I will never forget. I paid 50 PLN for my ticket to see a local jazz band, and it was worth every zloty.

For a different kind of vibe, SQ Klub (Półwiejska 42, 61-888 Poznań) offers a range of performances from live DJs to eclectic electronic acts. It's one of the city's top spots for modern beats. Drinks start around 15 PLN, but entrance fees can vary, usually around 40 PLN.

Coordinates: 52.4095° N, 16.9319° E

Opening Hours: Vary by venue, generally open from 7 PM - 2 AM for live performances.

13.3 Unique Nighttime Experiences: From Jazz to Karaoke

During my stay, I stumbled upon a hidden gem called Cooliozum (Zwierzyniecka 10, 60-813 Poznań). It's a karaoke bar that attracts locals and tourists alike. I'm usually shy about karaoke, but the crowd was so warm that I ended up belting out a few tunes. With beers priced at around 8 PLN, it's an affordable and fun way to spend the night.

Another unique experience is catching some live jazz at Dragon Social Club (Zamkowa 3, 61-768 Poznań). The relaxed, bohemian vibe makes it a great spot for jazz enthusiasts. I spent a mellow evening there with a glass of wine, soaking in some smooth melodies.

Coordinates: 52.4083° N, 16.9341° E

Opening Hours: 8 PM - 1 AM, later on weekends.

13.4 The Best Places for Cocktails and Craft Beers

I'm a sucker for a well-made cocktail, and Woda Ognista (Żydowska 6/7, 61-761 Poznań) had some of the best I've ever tasted. They specialize in Polish vodkas but craft them into modern cocktails. I tried the Zubrowka Sour, a mix of bison grass vodka and fresh herbs, for 25 PLN, and it was a revelation.

For craft beer, Ministerstwo Browaru (Wrocławska 8, 61-838 Poznań) was my go-to. The place boasts a wide range of local and international craft brews. You can try a pint for around 12-18 PLN, and trust me, the selection is extensive.

Coordinates: 52.4082° N, 16.9335° E

Opening Hours: Open from 5 PM - 2 AM daily.

13.5 Poznań by Night: A Safe and Fun Experience

I found Poznań to be very safe at night, especially in the Old Town. I was initially hesitant to wander the streets after dark, but the city is well-lit, and there's a visible police presence, particularly in the popular areas. Walking back to my hotel after a late night at Blue Note, I felt completely at ease, even at 2 AM. The locals were friendly and helpful, which added to the overall feeling of safety.

Chapter 14

How to Engage with Local Culture

14.1 Language: Key Polish Phrases for Travelers

I found that while many people in Poznań speak English, knowing a few basic Polish phrases definitely earned me some brownie points. The locals appreciated my attempts, and it made for a warmer experience. Here are some essentials:

"Dzień dobry" (Good morning)

"Dziękuję" (Thank you)

"Proszę" (Please)

"Przepraszam" (Excuse me/Sorry) The word I used the most? "Jak się masz?" which means "How are you?"—it always sparked a friendly response.

14.2 How to Participate in Local Traditions and Festivals

I had the pleasure of visiting Poznań during the Świętomarcińskie Rogale Festival, a celebration of St. Martin's croissants. The whole city came alive with parades, music, and of course, endless amounts of croissants filled with white poppy seeds and icing. It's held every year on November 11th, and it's a must-experience if you're in town. The croissants cost around 7-12 PLN depending on where you buy them, and they're incredibly delicious.

14.3 Meeting Locals: Poznań's Friendliest Neighborhoods

I spent a lot of time in the Jeżyce neighborhood, which I found to be one of the most welcoming areas in Poznań. It's a little off the beaten path, but its cozy cafes and local markets made it the perfect spot for interacting with locals. I made a friend at Kombinat (Kościelna 43, 60-537 Poznań), a small coffee shop where I spent a rainy afternoon. We ended up chatting for hours over some of the best coffee I've had in the city.

Coordinates: 52.4206° N, 16.9104° E

Opening Hours: Generally 8 AM - 6 PM.

14.4 Craft Workshops and Cultural Classes

I wanted to take home more than just memories, so I signed up for a pottery class at Sztukarnia (Sienkiewicza 22, 60-818 Poznań). It was a fantastic way to connect with the local art scene, and I even made my own handmade Polish ceramic piece! The workshop lasted about 3 hours and cost me 100 PLN. The class is conducted in Polish, but the instructors are patient and willing to translate where needed.

Coordinates: 52.4074° N, 16.9343° E

Opening Hours: Workshops available by booking.

14.5 Volunteering and Giving Back During Your Trip

During my stay, I decided to spend a day volunteering at the Poznań Volunteer Centre (Plac Wolności 18, 61-738 Poznań). They connect travelers with local volunteering opportunities, ranging from environmental work to helping out at cultural events. I joined a team working on a community garden project in the city's outskirts, which was an incredibly rewarding way to give back while connecting with locals.

Coordinates: 52.4085° N, 16.9331° E

Opening Hours: 9 AM - 5 PM (for the volunteer center)

Website: wolontariat.poznan.pl

Overall, my time in Poznań was a blend of nightlife thrills and meaningful cultural exchanges. From karaoke in a packed bar to getting my hands dirty in a community garden, Poznań gave me experiences that I'll cherish for years to come. And remember, whether you're belting out a song at Cooliozum or making a friend over coffee in Jeżyce, Poznań is a city that will embrace you if you take the time to embrace it back.

Chapter 15

Day Trips and Excursions from Poznań

Poznań is such a charming city with its blend of history, culture, and natural beauty, but sometimes it's the areas around a place that really bring its story to life. I've always found day trips to be the best way to dive into the region, and Poznań is no exception. Whether you're fascinated by palaces, curious about steam trains, or simply want to stretch your legs in the countryside, the areas surrounding Poznań offer unforgettable experiences.

15.1 Discovering the Wielkopolska Countryside

When I first ventured into the Wielkopolska countryside, I didn't know what to expect, but it ended up being one of the highlights of my time in Poznań. The landscape is a mix of lush forests, serene lakes, and charming villages. There's something uniquely peaceful about the open space, especially if you're used to the hustle of city life.

If you're into hiking, Wielkopolska National Park (Wielkopolski Park Narodowy) is just a short drive from Poznań, about 15 kilometers to the south (52.2448° N, 16.7573° E). The park has well-marked trails that wind through forests and around picturesque lakes. One of my favorite trails is the walk up to Glacial Hill, where the view over the surrounding fields and forests is breathtaking. The park is also home to several bird species, so it's great for birdwatching.

Opening Hours: Open 24/7 (the park itself)

Coordinates: 52.2448° N, 16.7573° E

Address: Jeziorna 7, 62-050 Mosina, Poland

Contact: +48 61 813 49 91

Price Range: Free entry (some areas may charge a small fee for parking)

If you want a deeper dive into rural Polish life, a visit to the Wielkopolska Ethnographic Park in Dziekanowice is a must. The open-air museum showcases traditional wooden homes, barns, and mills, giving you a real sense of what life was like here centuries ago. It's a place that made me reflect on the simple life, and I even had the chance to watch a traditional blacksmith at work.

Coordinates: 52.5936° N, 17.4591° E

Address: Dziekanowice, 62-261 Dziekanowice, Poland

Contact: +48 61 427 50 14

Price Range: Adult ticket: 10 PLN (~€2.20)

15.2 Exploring Rogalin Palace and Arboretum

Rogalin Palace (Pałac w Rogalinie) is one of those places that instantly transports you to another time. The first time I arrived at the palace, the grandeur of its Baroque architecture left me speechless. Built in the 18th century by the Raczyński family, it's a stunning example of aristocratic life. The interior is beautifully preserved, and the art gallery inside boasts an impressive collection of Polish paintings.

What made my visit even more special was the arboretum surrounding the palace. There are ancient oak trees here, some of which are over 1,000 years old, standing like silent sentinels of history. Walking through the grounds, I felt a deep connection to the past, like these trees had seen generations come and go, and now I was just one more traveler passing through.

Opening Hours: Tuesday to Sunday, 9 AM to 5 PM (Closed on Mondays)

Coordinates: 52.2679° N, 16.9686° E

Address: Plac Powstańców Wielkopolskich 2, 62-022 Rogalin, Poland

Contact: +48 61 813 82 10

Price Range: Adult ticket: 20 PLN (~€4.50)

Website Address: muzeum.raczynskich.pl

15.3 The Historic City of Gniezno

Gniezno is a city that's often overshadowed by Poznań, but for history buffs, it's an essential day trip. Located about 50 kilometers east of Poznań, Gniezno was once the capital of Poland and is considered the birthplace of the Polish state. As soon as I stepped into the Gniezno Cathedral (Katedra Gnieźnieńska), I could feel the weight of centuries of history. This Gothic cathedral is where Poland's first kings were crowned, and its bronze doors, decorated with scenes from the life of St. Adalbert, are nothing short of awe-inspiring.

If you're lucky, you might catch one of the organ concerts that take place here—it's a surreal experience listening to the music echo through the grand stone halls.

Opening Hours: Daily, 9 AM to 6 PM

Coordinates: 52.5350° N, 17.6007° E

Address: Katedra Gnieźnieńska, Wzgórze Lecha 2, 62-200 Gniezno, Poland

Contact: +48 61 426 14 67

Price Range: Adult ticket: 12 PLN (~€2.60)

15.4 Kórnik Castle: A Fairy Tale Experience

Kórnik Castle (Zamek w Kórniku) looks like something straight out of a fairy tale. Located about 25 kilometers southeast of Poznań, the castle is a neo-Gothic masterpiece surrounded by a moat and lush gardens. When I visited, I felt like I'd stepped into a storybook. Inside, the rooms are filled with antique furniture, and the library is particularly impressive, housing thousands of rare books.

The gardens outside the castle are perfect for a stroll, and there's even a picturesque arboretum. It's the kind of place where you can lose yourself in thought, imagining the people who lived there centuries ago.

Opening Hours: Tuesday to Sunday, 10 AM to 4 PM (Closed on Mondays)

Coordinates: 52.2456° N, 17.0868° E

Address: Zamkowa 5, 62-035 Kórnik, Poland

Contact: +48 61 817 00 81

Price Range: Adult ticket: 15 PLN (~€3.30)

Website Address: kornik.pl

15.5 Day Trip to Wolsztyn and Its Steam Locomotive Depot

If you're a fan of old steam trains, Wolsztyn is an absolute must. It's about an hour and a half drive from Poznań (96 kilometers), and the Wolsztyn Steam Locomotive Depot is the last place in Europe where steam trains still run on regular timetables. The sight and sound of these old engines chugging along the tracks is something I'll never forget.

There's a museum attached to the depot that walks you through the history of steam trains in Poland. But the real thrill comes when you step onto one of these vintage locomotives for a ride through the countryside. I'll never forget the feeling of the steam blowing past me and the rhythmic clatter of the wheels on the tracks.

Opening Hours: Daily, 10 AM to 4 PM

Coordinates: 52.1156° N, 16.1283° E

Address: Fabryczna 1, 64-200 Wolsztyn, Poland

Contact: +48 68 384 20 29

Price Range: Entry: 10 PLN (~€2.20)

Website Address: parowozowniawolsztyn.pl

This is just a slice of what the Poznań region has to offer. Each of these trips gave me new perspectives on Poland's rich history and natural beauty. By the time I returned to the city, I felt like I'd not only visited another country but also walked through time. If you're looking for day trips from Poznań, any of these destinations will leave you with unforgettable memories.

Chapter 16

Family-Friendly Activities

Poznań is a fantastic city for families. During my stay, I traveled with my nieces and nephews, and I was impressed by the variety of activities available for kids. Whether your family enjoys exploring the outdoors, interactive learning, or simply having fun at amusement parks, Poznań has something for every age group. Here are some of the top family-friendly things to do in the city.

16.1 Top Attractions for Kids

One of the first places I took the kids was Poznań Croissant Museum (Rogalowe Muzeum Poznania), and it ended up being one of the highlights of our trip. The museum, located in the Old Market Square, is dedicated to the city's famous St. Martin's Croissant (rogal świętomarciński), and kids get the chance to make their own croissants in a fun and interactive workshop. My nieces were thrilled to be wearing little chef hats and kneading the dough. I have to say, the smell of fresh pastry baking was almost as delightful as the experience itself. It's a fun, hands-on way to learn about local culture, and the croissants are delicious!

Opening Hours: Daily, 11 AM to 5 PM

Coordinates: 52.4085° N, 16.9348° E

Address: Stary Rynek 41/2, 61-772 Poznań, Poland

Contact: +48 61 307 07 27

Price Range: Adult ticket: 19 PLN (€4.20), Child ticket: 16 PLN (€3.50)

Website Address: rogalowemuzeum.pl

Another great spot for children is Malta Ski, which isn't just a ski slope but a whole recreational area with year-round activities. In the summer, there's a roller coaster, mini-golf, and even a summer tubing track. The kids loved the roller coaster that winds its way down the hill overlooking Malta Lake. In winter, Malta Ski becomes a ski and snowboarding park, and although it's not the Alps, it's perfect for beginners or a fun family outing. We spent an entire afternoon there, and the kids had a blast racing down the hill on inflatable tubes.

Opening Hours: Daily, 10 AM to 8 PM (varies by season)

Coordinates: 52.4072° N, 16.9761° E

Address: Wiankowa 2, 61-131 Poznań, Poland

Contact: +48 61 877 05 52

Price Range: Activities range from 10-40 PLN (~€2.20 - €8.80)

Website Address: maltaski.pl

16.2 Family-Friendly Restaurants and Cafés

Traveling with kids also means finding places to eat that are family-friendly. One of our go-to spots was Manekin—a restaurant chain that specializes in pancakes, both savory and sweet. The portions are generous, and they have a children's menu that offers simple, familiar options like pancakes with Nutella or chicken strips. It's a great place to stop for lunch or a quick snack when you're exploring the city.

Coordinates: 52.4064° N, 16.9299° E

Address: ul. Kwiatowa 3, 61-881 Poznań, Poland

Contact: +48 61 307 01 09

Price Range: Main dishes: 20-30 PLN (~€4.40 - €6.60)

Website Address: manekin.pl

For a more unique experience, we took the kids to Papierówka, a quirky little café in the Jeżyce neighborhood. It has a dedicated play area for young children, complete with toys and books. The relaxed atmosphere was perfect for grabbing a coffee while the kids were entertained. The menu features healthy snacks like smoothies, salads, and delicious sandwiches.

Coordinates: 52.4128° N, 16.9072° E

Address: ul. Dąbrowskiego 42, 60-840 Poznań, Poland

Contact: +48 61 307 97 31

Price Range: Snacks and drinks: 15-25 PLN (~€3.30 - €5.50)

Website Address: papierowka-jezyce.pl

16.3 Amusement Parks and Playgrounds

A bit outside the city is Rodzinny Park Rozrywki (Family Amusement Park), which we visited for a full day of fun. The park features various rides, including carousels, bumper cars, and even a small Ferris wheel. My nephew's favorite was the pirate ship ride, while my niece couldn't get enough of the giant slides. There's also a playground area with swings and climbing frames, making it a great spot to let the kids run around while you take a break.

Opening Hours: Monday to Friday, 10 AM to 6 PM; Weekends, 10 AM to 8 PM

Coordinates: 52.3835° N, 16.8304° E

Address: ul. Bałtycka 10, 62-030 Luboń, Poland

Contact: +48 61 292 05 84

Price Range: Entry: 30 PLN (~€6.60) per person

Website Address: parkrodzinny.pl

If you're looking for something closer to the city, Citadel Park (Park Cytadela) is a beautiful spot with wide open spaces, perfect for a family picnic or a casual walk. There's a great playground within the park that's divided into sections for different age groups. While the kids were playing, I had a chance to wander around and check out the sculptures and memorials scattered throughout the park, which was once a military fort.

Opening Hours: Open 24/7

Coordinates: 52.4219° N, 16.9309° E

Address: Al. Armii Poznań, 61-626 Poznań, Poland

Price Range: Free entry

16.4 Educational Experiences for Curious Young Minds

One of the most memorable places we visited was the Brama Poznania Interactive Heritage Center. It's an interactive museum that tells the story of the city's history in a way that's engaging for both kids and adults. Using multimedia exhibits, the museum explores the origins of Poznań and the history of the Ostrow Tumski area. My nieces enjoyed playing with the touchscreen exhibits and listening to the audio guides tailored for kids.

Opening Hours: Tuesday to Sunday, 10 AM to 6 PM (Closed Mondays)

Coordinates: 52.4124° N, 16.9530° E

Address: ul. Gdańska 2, 61-123 Poznań, Poland

Contact: +48 61 647 76 34

Price Range: Adult ticket: 15 PLN (€3.30), Child ticket: 8 PLN (€1.80)

Website Address: bramapoznania.pl

Another educational gem is The Poznań Palm House (Palmiarnia Poznańska). It's the perfect place to escape the city and dive into a tropical world. The Palm House is one of the largest in Europe and features thousands of plant species from all over the globe. My nephews were fascinated by the fish ponds and the colorful birds that live in the greenhouse. The whole experience felt like a mini-jungle adventure, right in the heart of Poznań.

Opening Hours: Tuesday to Sunday, 9 AM to 5 PM (Closed Mondays)

Coordinates: 52.3948° N, 16.8903° E

Address: ul. Matejki 18, 60-771 Poznań, Poland

Contact: +48 61 865 89 64

Price Range: Adult ticket: 12 PLN (€2.60), Child ticket: 8 PLN (€1.80)

Website Address: palmiarnia.poznan.pl

16.5 Poznań Zoo and Other Animal Attractions

No family trip is complete without a visit to the Poznań Zoo (Nowe Zoo), and this one is a real treat. It's one of the largest zoos in Poland, spread over a vast area near Malta Lake. We rented a small electric cart to get around (which was a great idea with kids), and it took us through exhibits featuring everything from elephants to lynxes. The highlight for the kids was the giraffe enclosure, where they got to see these majestic animals up close.

What I loved most about this zoo was its focus on conservation. Many of the animals here are endangered species, and the zoo does a great job of educating visitors about the importance of protecting wildlife.

Opening Hours: Daily, 9 AM to 7 PM (varies by season)

Coordinates: 52.4044° N, 16.9914° E

Address: Krańcowa 81, 61-037 Poznań, Poland

Contact: +48 61 877 35 02

Price Range: Adult ticket: 30 PLN (€6.60), Child ticket: 20 PLN (€4.40)

Website Address: zoo.poznan.pl

For a smaller, more intimate experience, the Old Zoo (Stare Zoo) in the city center is also worth a visit. It's free to enter, and although it's much smaller than the Nowe Zoo, it's a charming place with a focus on smaller animals like reptiles, birds, and small mammals. It's perfect for younger children who might not have the stamina for a whole day at the bigger zoo.

Opening Hours: Daily, 9 AM to 7 PM

Coordinates: 52.4094° N, 16.9112° E

Address: ul. Zwierzyniecka 19, 60-814 Poznań, Poland

Contact: +48 61 877 35 02

Price Range: Free entry

This chapter, focused on family-friendly activities, brings out the best Poznań has to offer for travelers with children. From fun interactive museums and animal encounters to outdoor adventures and great dining spots, Poznań makes family travel easy and enjoyable. Each place I visited with my family left us with a deeper appreciation for the city's welcoming nature, and I'm sure it will for you too.

Chapter 17

Practical Information

Every time I travel, I realize just how important it is to be prepared with practical details. Poznań, while welcoming and easy to navigate, has a few quirks you'll want to be aware of to make your trip as hassle-free as possible. This chapter is all about those everyday things you might not think about until you need them: where to exchange money, how to access Wi-Fi, and what to do in case of an emergency.

17.1 Currency Exchange and ATMs

Poland uses the Polish złoty (PLN), and while most places in Poznań accept credit and debit cards, it's always a good idea to have some cash on hand, especially for smaller shops or local markets. During my visit, I found that it was easiest to withdraw money directly from ATMs using my bank card, as the exchange rates were generally more favorable than those at currency exchange offices.

ATMs (called bankomat in Polish) are widely available throughout the city, especially in popular areas like the Old Market Square (Stary Rynek) and major shopping districts. Some of the most reliable banks with ATMs include PKO Bank Polski, Santander, and ING. Most ATMs offer instructions in English, and withdrawing cash with a foreign card is straightforward.

If you prefer to exchange currency, there are several kantors (currency exchange offices) around the city. I found the Kantor in the Old Market Square to offer competitive rates and fast service.

Address of Kantor: Stary Rynek 50, 61-772 Poznań, Poland

Coordinates: 52.4086° N, 16.9342° E

Price Range: Varies by exchange rate (no commission at most kantors)

Tip: Avoid exchanging money at airports or train stations, as the rates are usually much worse.

17.2 Internet, Wi-Fi, and SIM Cards

Staying connected in Poznań is easy, and you'll find free Wi-Fi in many public places, such as cafés, restaurants, shopping malls, and even in some parks. The Poznań Wi-Fi network, available in parts of the city, was quite reliable during my stay, especially in tourist-heavy areas like the Old Market Square and along the Warta River.

If you're staying for a few days or need more reliable internet access, I recommend picking up a Polish SIM card. I grabbed mine from Orange, one of the major telecom providers in Poland, and it was a breeze to set up. You can buy a prepaid SIM card at the airport, convenience stores, or mobile shops around the city. Most packages come with data plans, and prices are very affordable compared to other European countries.

Address of Orange Store: ul. Półwiejska 42, 61-888 Poznań, Poland

Coordinates: 52.4042° N, 16.9249° E

Price Range: Prepaid SIM with data starting from 20 PLN (~€4.40)

Website Address: orange.pl

Tip: Make sure your phone is unlocked before purchasing a local SIM card.

17.3 Health Services and Pharmacies

I didn't need to use medical services during my stay, but I always like to know where the nearest clinic or pharmacy is, just in case. Poznań has a modern healthcare system, and most clinics and hospitals are well-equipped to handle emergencies. Many doctors and healthcare staff speak English, so communication shouldn't be a major issue.

For minor illnesses, you can easily find pharmacies (apteki) all around the city. There's a good one located right in the city center that I passed by several times during my stay. Pharmacies are usually open from 9 AM to 6 PM on weekdays, though some are open late or 24/7.

Address of Apteka: ul. Półwiejska 42, 61-888 Poznań, Poland

Coordinates: 52.4042° N, 16.9252° E

Contact: +48 61 852 48 99

Price Range: Varies based on medication; many over-the-counter medicines are very affordable.

If you need more serious medical attention, the Poznań University of Medical Sciences Hospital is a major hospital and provides high-quality care. It's where I would have gone if I had needed medical help during my trip.

Address of Hospital: ul. Przybyszewskiego 49, 60-355 Poznań, Poland

Coordinates: 52.4021° N, 16.8937° E

Contact: +48 61 869 10 00

Website Address: umed.pl

Tip: It's always a good idea to travel with basic first aid supplies and any prescription medications you may need, as well as travel insurance that covers healthcare abroad.

17.4 Emergency Contacts and Numbers

In case of an emergency, it's crucial to know how to get help quickly. Poland uses the European Union's standard emergency number, 112, which will connect you to emergency services like police, fire, and medical help. Fortunately, I never had to use it, but it's reassuring to know that English-speaking operators are available.

Here's a list of key emergency numbers you should keep handy while in Poznań:

Emergency Number (Police, Fire, Ambulance): 112

Police (local): 997

Fire Department: 998

Ambulance Service: 999

Tourist Information Center: +48 61 852 61 56 (located in the Old Market Square)

During my stay, I also kept the contact info for the nearest embassy or consulate of my country just in case I needed assistance. If you're not sure where yours is located, the tourist information center can usually help you find it.

17.5 Tipping Etiquette in Poznań

Tipping in Poland is generally appreciated but not mandatory. When dining at restaurants, it's common to leave a 10% to 15% tip if the service was good. In more casual places, rounding up the bill is also perfectly acceptable. During my time in Poznań, I found that tipping wasn't expected at cafés or bars, though I would sometimes leave a little extra if the service was exceptional.

Here are a few general guidelines for tipping in Poznań:

Restaurants: 10-15% of the bill

Taxis: Round up to the nearest 5 PLN

Hotel Staff: A small tip (around 5-10 PLN) for bellhops or housekeeping is appreciated, though not obligatory

Tour Guides: 10-20 PLN (~€2.20-€4.40) per person for group tours

It's also worth noting that in some restaurants, you may be asked if you want to include a tip when paying by card. Make sure to clarify this with your server, as it's easier to leave a cash tip directly if you're unsure.

This chapter on practical information should give you all the tools you need to navigate Poznań like a local. From knowing where to exchange money and how to stay connected to understanding Poland's tipping customs, these details will make your stay more comfortable and stress-free.

I remember feeling so much more relaxed once I had these basics covered, and it allowed me to enjoy all the fun activities and adventures Poznań has to offer without any worries.

Chapter 18

Poznań on a Budget

Exploring Poznań without breaking the bank was one of the best parts of my time in this vibrant Polish city. With its rich history, beautiful architecture, and lively atmosphere, you can experience plenty without spending a fortune. I found that blending free attractions with affordable dining, and using smart travel hacks, made my stay both memorable and budget-friendly.

18.1 Free or Low-Cost Attractions

One of the highlights of my trip was walking through the Old Market Square (Stary Rynek). It's absolutely free, and the beautiful Renaissance town hall, with its famous goat clock display at noon, is a sight you can't miss. Watching the mechanical goats butt heads was surprisingly entertaining! I'd recommend taking a stroll through the surrounding streets to admire the colorful facades of the old merchant houses. The square is alive with history and local energy, especially during warmer months.

I also enjoyed spending time in Cytadela Park, which is the largest park in the city and a wonderful spot to relax or have a picnic. Not only is it free, but the park also features sculptures and remnants of the fortifications from its military past. I even stumbled upon the Poznań Army Museum, which is located within the park and has free entry.

Coordinates: 52.4095° N, 16.9319° E

Address: Aleja Niepodległości, 61-713 Poznań

18.2 Affordable Dining and Street Food

When it came to affordable eats, I fell in love with Zapiekanki, which is essentially a Polish-style open-faced sandwich. I grabbed one at a street vendor near the market square for just 10 PLN (about $2.50), and it was huge and satisfying. There are also plenty of budget-friendly milk bars (Bary Mleczne), where you can get traditional Polish dishes like pierogi for a few dollars. Bar Pod Arkadami was one of my favorite spots for a cheap and hearty meal.

Address: Stary Rynek 56, 61-772 Poznań

Price range: 10–30 PLN ($2.50–$7)

18.3 Budget-Friendly Accommodation

I stayed at Hostel Poco Loco during my visit, which was both affordable and centrally located. It's a great option if you're traveling on a budget but still want to be close to everything. For under $20 a night, I had access to a comfortable bed, free Wi-Fi, and a shared kitchen, which helped me save on meals.

Address: Taczaka 23, 61-819 Poznań

Phone Number: +48 61 307 06 12

Price range: 70–100 PLN ($17–$25)

website: poclocohostel.pl

18.4 Money-Saving Tips for Transportation

Getting around Poznań is relatively cheap if you know the tricks. I made good use of the city's Poznań Public Transport system, which offers single tickets for around 4.60 PLN (a little over $1), but the real deal is the 24-hour pass, which only costs about 15 PLN (roughly $3.50). This is perfect if you plan on exploring various parts of the city in one day.

Additionally, I found that renting a bike through Nextbike was an enjoyable and affordable way to explore. It's free for the first 20 minutes, and after that, it costs just 1 PLN for every 20 minutes, which makes it a great option for short trips around the city.

website: nextbike.pl

18.5 Best Ways to Enjoy Poznań for Less

To get the most out of Poznań without spending much, I recommend visiting on foot or by bike to soak in the local atmosphere. Keep an eye out for free walking tours, which often start from the Old Market Square, and offer insightful overviews of the city's history and culture. Don't forget to check out the free days at museums, like The National Museum, which offers free entry on Tuesdays.

Chapter 19

Festivals and Events in Poznań

I was lucky enough to time my visit with St. Martin's Day, and it made the experience truly unforgettable. Poznań hosts a variety of festivals throughout the year, and each event offers a unique window into the local culture and traditions.

19.1 St. Martin's Day and the Famous Parade

St. Martin's Day, celebrated every November 11th, is one of Poznań's most iconic events. The streets come alive with a vibrant parade that starts on Święty Marcin Street (St. Martin Street), and the highlight is the traditional St. Martin's croissant (rogale świętomarcińskie), a sweet, crescent-shaped pastry filled with poppy seeds and nuts. I couldn't resist trying one (or two!), and it was worth every calorie.

Address: Święty Marcin Street, Poznań

Price range (croissant): 10–15 PLN ($2.50–$4)

19.2 The International Theatre Festival

The Malta Festival Poznań, held every June, is a celebration of theatre, music, and performance art. What's great is that many events are free, especially the outdoor performances in Plac Wolności (Liberty Square). I attended a few shows there and was blown away by the creativity and talent. The festival attracts artists from all over Europe, making it a cultural feast for anyone visiting during this time.

Address: Plac Wolności, Poznań

Dates: Annually in June

19.3 Christmas Markets and Winter Magic

Visiting Poznań during Christmas is magical. The Poznań Bethlehem Market, held in the Old Market Square and Plac Wolności, is a winter wonderland with festive stalls, holiday treats, and an ice rink. I enjoyed sipping on mulled wine while browsing the handcrafted ornaments and gifts.

Address: Stary Rynek, Poznań

Dates: Late November to December

Price range: Free entry (small costs for food and drink)

19.4 Summer Music Festivals

Poznań comes alive in the summer with music festivals like Enter Enea Festival, which takes place by Lake Strzeszyńskie. The outdoor setting, combined with live jazz performances, made for a perfect summer evening. Tickets are affordable, and I highly recommend it for music lovers.

Address: Jezioro Strzeszyńskie, Poznań

Price range: 70–150 PLN ($17–$35)

19.5 Poznań International Fair

If you're in town for business or just enjoy large events, the Poznań International Fair is a hub for trade shows and exhibitions. It's one of the largest fairgrounds in Europe, and whether you're into cars, food, or fashion, there's likely something happening during your visit.

Address: Głogowska 14, 60-734 Poznań

Phone Number: +48 61 869 2000

website: mpt.poznan.pl

Chapter 20

Insider Tips for the Best Experience

After spending time exploring Poznań, I picked up a few insider tips that really enhanced my experience and helped me navigate the city like a local.

20.1 How to Avoid Crowds at Popular Sites

The best way to avoid the crowds at popular sites like the Old Market Square is to go early in the morning or late in the afternoon, especially during the summer. I found the square to be quieter around 9 AM, allowing me to enjoy the architecture without the throngs of tourists.

20.2 Local Secrets: Hidden Gems Worth Discovering

One of the best hidden gems I found was Brama Poznania ICHOT, an interactive museum dedicated to the history of Poznań. It's not as well-known as other attractions, but it provides a fantastic overview of the city's origins. Plus, the surrounding area near Ostrów Tumski is beautiful for a quiet walk.

Address: Gdańska 2, 61-123 Poznań

Price: 20 PLN ($5)

website: bramapoznania.pl

20.3 How to Save Time with Skip-the-Line Tickets

For some of Poznań's more popular attractions, like Palmiarnia Poznańska (Poznań Palm House), I recommend booking skip-the-line tickets online. This saved me a lot of time, especially during the busy summer months.

Address: Matejki 18, 60-767 Poznań

Price range: 12–20 PLN ($3–$5)

website: palmiarnia.poznan.pl

20.4 Unique Local Experiences Off the Beaten Path

For a truly local experience, I suggest taking a day trip to the Rogalin Palace and its ancient oak trees. This is a bit off the beaten path, but worth it if you enjoy history and nature.

Address: Rogalińska 5, 62-022 Rogalin

Price: 30 PLN ($7)

website: muzeumrogalin.pl

20.5 Best Apps and Websites for Poznań Travelers

Before heading out, I downloaded the Jakdojade app, which made navigating Poznań's public transport a breeze. I also used Zomato to find affordable restaurants based on reviews.

Looking back, I realize how much I managed to see and experience in Poznań without spending a fortune. From attending festivals like St. Martin's Day to discovering local secrets and using smart travel tips, it was an adventure I'll never forget!

Appendix

In this appendix, I've compiled all the essential information you might need during your stay in Poznań. From emergency contacts to maps, addresses of popular spots, and important health services, this chapter will serve as your go-to reference.

A. Emergency Contacts

Having emergency contact information is critical during any trip. Here are the numbers you need to keep handy while in Poznań:

General Emergency Number (Police, Fire, Ambulance): 112

Police: 997

Fire Department: 998

Ambulance: 999

Tourist Information Center (Old Market Square): +48 61 852 61 56

Poznań University of Medical Sciences Hospital: +48 61 869 10 00

Address: ul. Przybyszewskiego 49, 60-355 Poznań

Coordinates: 52.4021° N, 16.8937° E

B. Maps and Navigational Tools

Navigating Poznań is relatively easy, but here are a few tips and tools to help you get around more efficiently:

Google Maps: Always a reliable choice for navigating the city, finding restaurants, attractions, and getting directions.

JakDojadę: A useful app for public transport schedules, available in English and Polish. It shows tram, bus, and metro routes and times.

Poznań Public Transport Map: Available at most kiosks or online at ztm.poznan.pl, it shows detailed routes for trams and buses.

Offline Maps: If you're worried about data usage, download an offline map of Poznań from Google Maps before your trip.

Map of Things to do in Poznań

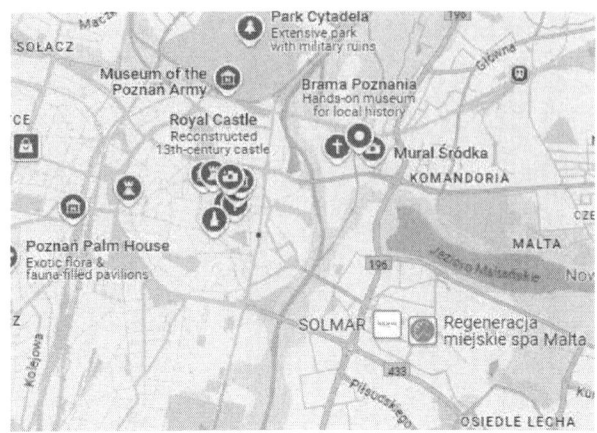

https://www.google.com/maps/search/Things+to+do/@52.4089153,16.8612589,13z/data=!3m1!4b1?entry=ttu&g_ep=EgoyMDI0MDkwMi4xIKXMDSoASAFQAw%3D%3D

SCAN THE IMAGE/QR CODE WITH YOUR PHONE TO GET THE LOCATIONS IN REAL TIME.

C. Useful Local Phrases

While many people in Poznań speak English, especially in tourist areas, knowing a few Polish phrases can go a long way in making your trip smoother and more enjoyable. Here are some helpful words and phrases:

Hello: Cześć (cheshch)

Good morning: Dzień dobry (jen DOH-brih)

Goodbye: Do widzenia (doh veed-ZEH-nya)

Please: Proszę (PROH-sheh)

Thank you: Dziękuję (jen-KOO-yeh)

Yes: Tak (tahk)

No: Nie (nyeh)

Excuse me: Przepraszam (psheh-PRAH-shahm)

How much does it cost?: Ile to kosztuje? (EE-leh toh koh-sh-TOO-yeh)

Where is…?: Gdzie jest…? (g-JEH yest)

D. Addresses and Locations of Popular Accommodation

Here are some of the top recommended places to stay in Poznań, ranging from luxury hotels to budget-friendly options.

Sheraton Poznań Hotel

Address: ul. Bukowska 3/9, 60-809 Poznań

Coordinates: 52.4108° N, 16.9097° E

Phone: +48 61 655 20 00

PURO Hotel Poznań

Address: ul. Stawna 12, 61-759 Poznań

Coordinates: 52.4115° N, 16.9342° E

Phone: +48 61 333 10 00

Blooms Boutique Hostel

Address: ul. Kwiatowa 2, 61-881 Poznań

Coordinates: 52.4048° N, 16.9274° E

Phone: +48 61 224 30 15

Ibis Poznań Stare Miasto

Address: ul. Kazimierza Wielkiego 23, 61-863 Poznań

Coordinates: 52.4023° N, 16.9381° E

Phone: +48 61 858 44 00

E. Addresses and Locations of Popular Restaurants and Cafés

Poznań is brimming with great places to eat and drink. Here are a few top choices:

Manekin (Pancake Restaurant)

Address: ul. Kwiatowa 3, 61-881 Poznań

Coordinates: 52.4064° N, 16.9299° E

Phone: +48 61 307 01 09

Wypieki Cafe

Address: ul. Wroniecka 23, 61-763 Poznań

Coordinates: 52.4107° N, 16.9359° E

Phone: +48 793 707 074

Brovaria Restaurant & Brewery

Address: Stary Rynek 73, 61-772 Poznań

Coordinates: 52.4084° N, 16.9345° E

Phone: +48 61 858 68 68

F. Addresses and Locations of Popular Bars and Clubs

Whether you want a quiet drink or a night out, here are some favorite spots in Poznań:

Pijalnia Wódki i Piwa

Address: ul. Wrocławska 9, 61-838 Poznań

Coordinates: 52.4066° N, 16.9355° E

Phone: +48 609 756 678

Dragon Social Club

Address: ul. Zamkowa 3, 61-768 Poznań

Coordinates: 52.4090° N, 16.9341° E

Phone: +48 61 855 37 15

Mikrobar & Garden

Address: ul. Wodna 9, 61-781 Poznań

Coordinates: 52.4074° N, 16.9368° E

Phone: +48 518 518 949

G. Addresses and Locations of Top Attractions

Here are some of the must-see places in Poznań, covering history, culture, and natural beauty:

Stary Rynek (Old Market Square)

Coordinates: 52.4085° N, 16.9348° E

Address: Stary Rynek, 61-772 Poznań

Poznań Town Hall and the Famous Goats

Coordinates: 52.4084° N, 16.9342° E

Address: Stary Rynek 1, 61-768 Poznań

Phone: +48 61 878 52 31

Malta Lake

Coordinates: 52.4076° N, 16.9735° E

Address: ul. Wiankowa 3, 61-131 Poznań

Imperial Castle (Zamek Cesarski)

Coordinates: 52.4093° N, 16.9228° E

Address: ul. Święty Marcin 80/82, 61-809 Poznań

Phone: +48 61 659 92 00

H. Addresses and Locations of Book Shops

Poznań has a vibrant literary scene. If you're a book lover, here are a few places to pick up something to read:

Księgarnia Arsenał

Address: ul. Stary Rynek 41/42, 61-772 Poznań

Coordinates: 52.4090° N, 16.9341° E

Phone: +48 61 852 62 52

Bookowski - Księgarnia w Zamku

Address: ul. Święty Marcin 80/82, 61-809 Poznań (inside Imperial Castle)

Coordinates: 52.4093° N, 16.9228° E

Phone: +48 609 757 550

Księgarnia z Bajki

Address: ul. Lwa 2, 60-342 Poznań

Coordinates: 52.4099° N, 16.8531° E

Phone: +48 61 662 53 00

I. Addresses and Locations of Top Clinics, Hospitals, and Pharmacies

Health services in Poznań are reliable and accessible. Here are a few important places to know:

Poznań University of Medical Sciences Hospital

Address: ul. Przybyszewskiego 49, 60-355 Poznań

Coordinates: 52.4021° N, 16.8937° E

Phone: +48 61 869 10 00

Apteka (Pharmacy) Półwiejska

Address: ul. Półwiejska 42, 61-888 Poznań

Coordinates: 52.4042° N, 16.9252° E

Phone: +48 61 852 48 99

Apteka Św. Jana

Address: ul. Dąbrowskiego 32, 60-842 Poznań

Coordinates: 52.4095° N, 16.9086° E

Phone: +48 61 847 13 47

J. Addresses and Locations of UNESCO World Heritage Sites

While Poznań itself doesn't have any UNESCO World Heritage sites, Poland is home to many, some of which are close enough for day trips:

Torun Old Town

Address: Toruń, Poland (about 140 km from Poznań)

Coordinates: 53.0100° N, 18.6057° E

Wooden Churches of Southern Little Poland (Dębno, Binarowa)

Address: Binarowa, Poland (about 350 km from Poznań)

Coordinates: 49.7872° N, 20.9354° E

Centennial Hall in Wrocław

Address: Wrocław, Poland (about 175 km from Poznań)

Coordinates: 51.1087° N, 17.0764° E

Photo/Image Attribution

https://www.freepik.com/free-photo/old-church_919219.htm#fromView=search&page=1&position=0&uuid=c41570a6-d758-4050-8a4c-19395e2050ae

https://www.freepik.com/free-photo/clean-city-streets-prague_26732075.htm#fromView=search&page=1&position=2&uuid=56f53cff-f782-45d8-b41f-2250eb6e74aa

https://commons.wikimedia.org/wiki/File:Brama_Poznania_ICHOT_25-05-2014_01.jpg

https://upload.wikimedia.org/wikipedia/commons/4/40/Rogal_%C5%9Bwi%C4%99tomarci%C5%84ski_02.jpg

https://upload.wikimedia.org/wikipedia/commons/0/09/Playground_Cytadela_Poznan%2C_Tarasy.JPG

https://upload.wikimedia.org/wikipedia/commons/a/a6/Wielkopolski_National_Park_%28meadow%29.jpg

https://upload.wikimedia.org/wikipedia/commons/5/54/Bitllets_de_banc_polonesos_2024.jpg

https://upload.wikimedia.org/wikipedia/commons/8/84/Collage_of_views_of_Pozna%C5%84%2C_Poland.jpg

Printed in Great Britain
by Amazon